OSPREY COMBAT AIRCRAFT • 58

US NAVY HORNET UNITS OF OPERATION *IRAQI FREEDOM* PART TWO

SERIES EDITOR: TONY HOLMES

OSPREY COMBAT AIRCRAFT • 58

US NAVY HORNET UNITS OF OPERATION *IRAQI FREEDOM* PART TWO

TONY HOLMES

OSPREY

PUBLISHING

Front cover
Exemplifying the Hornet pilot's mantra in OIF that he or she was prepared to do virtually anything to save a fellow soldier in trouble on the ground, CVW-3's deputy air wing commander (DCAG) Capt Pat Rainey got 'down in the weeds' in northern Iraq in early April 2003 to help a Forward Air Controller escape enemy troops. Capt Rainey subsequently recounted the action to the author;

'I participated in a strike on the Mosul research facility with JDAM. My wingman on this mission was a "JO" (junior officer) from VFA-37, and after we had "Winchestered" (dropped) our bombs and were heading out of the target area, a FAC got onto our airborne controller, screaming for help. We told the controller that all we had left were 20 mm cannon rounds.

'The weather was a little iffy, and he was situated along the green line. He had been pinned down by a group of Iraqi soldiers. There was a ridgeline, with a road running along the top of it, a river at the base of the ridgeline and a bridge that spanned the river. He was pinned in the neck of this ridgeline where it met the bridge, and he couldn't get out. The FAC also had the Iraqis trapped on the other side of the bridge, and they couldn't get across to him thanks to the Navy air power in the area that was keeping them at bay. However, between passes by the Navy jets, they had been able to reposition themselves much closer to the bridge itself. We told the FAC that we only had 20 mm rounds, so we really couldn't help him, but he replied that we could help him a lot!

'We ended up coming in at the Iraqis from the back side of the ridgeline, which meant that they never saw us. We each completed a single strafing pass and the FAC was able to escape. We used the ridgeline to mask our approach, having first climbed to altitude to spot the enemy, who thought that we had departed the area. Once we popped up over the ridgeline we could clearly see the vehicles that the Iraqi troops were in – a couple of white SUVs and a BMP. There were probably between 60 and 70 soldiers in revetments sited around the bridge. They had also hastily erected some kind of fortification, including a burned-out car, and pushed it up as a barrier at one end of the bridge. About a mile away they were massing a force in preparation for an assault on the bridge. Our strafing passes provided the FAC with the breathing space he required to effect his escape.'

In this specially commissioned artwork created by Mark Postlethwaite, Capt Rainey can be seen just seconds away from pulling up over the ridgeline and commencing his strafing run in VFA-37's F/A-18C Hornet 'Bull 300' (BuNo 165181)

First published in Great Britain in 2005 by Osprey Publishing
Midland House, West Way, Botley, Oxford OX2 0PH, UK
443 Park Avenue South, New York, NY 10016, USA
E-mail:info@ospreypublishing.com

© 2005 Osprey Publishing Limited

ISBN 1 84176 885 5

Written & Edited by Tony Holmes
Page Design by Tony Truscott
Cover Artwork by Mark Postlethwaite
Aircraft Profiles by Chris Davey
Index by Alison Worthington
Originated by PPS-Grasmere, Leeds, UK
Printed in China through Bookbuilders

05 06 07 08 09   10 09 08 07 06 05 04 03 02 01

For a catalogue of all books published by Osprey please contact:
NORTH AMERICA
Osprey direct, 2427 Bond Street, University Park, IL 60466, USA
E-mail: info@ospreydirectusa,com

ALL OTHER REGIONS
Osprey Direct UK, P.O. Box 140 Wellingborough, Northants, NN8 2FA, UK
E-mail: info@ospreydirect.co.uk
www.ospreypublishing.com

EDITOR'S NOTE
To make this best-selling series as authoritative as possible, the Editor would be interested in hearing from any individual who may have relevant photographs, documentation or first-hand experiences relating to the world's elite pilots, and their aircraft, of the various theatres of war. Any material used will be credited to its original source. Please write to Tony Holmes via e-mail at:
tonyholmes67@yahoo.co.uk

CONTENTS

INTRODUCTION

As I wrote in the introduction to *US Navy Hornet Units of Operation Iraqi Freedom Part One*, the 2003 conflict in Iraq was dubbed by many TACAIR insiders the 'Hornet's War'. This was very much the case in the northern campaign, where the F/A-18 equipped four frontline light strike units, one reserve-manned squadron and a Marine Corps unit (the contribution made by the latter squadron, VMFA-115, to the war is covered in a companion volume). The 72 Hornets operating from the two aircraft carriers sailing in the eastern Mediterranean bore the brunt of the TACAIR mission in northern Iraq, and this volume tells the story of how this truly remarkable campaign was fought by the F/A-18 pilots assigned to this theatre.

Although somewhat overshadowed by the lightning war fought by the light strike units in the south, the Hornet squadrons in the north proved beyond a doubt just how effective tactical air power can be when you control the skies. This had been the case in Operation *Enduring Freedom* (OEF) 18 months earlier, and the lessons learned in Afghanistan were implemented over and over again in OIF's northern campaign. During the 30 days of conflict in northern Iraq the Hornet carried out virtually every TACAIR mission imaginable, attacking all manner of targets scattered across the region.

Acknowledgements

A significant number of naval aviators who flew the Hornet into combat from USS *Theodore Roosevelt* (CVN-71) and USS *Harry S Truman* (CVN-75) in OIF have made a contribution to this book, and the finished volume is considerably better for their valued input. Access to the men and women of the US armed forces who are currently engaged in the War on Terror has tightened up considerably in the post-9/11 world that we now live in. However, thanks to the personnel who man the US Navy's Chief of Naval Information (CHINFO) News Desk in the Pentagon, I was able to meet and interview key Hornet aircrew soon after they returned home from OIF. I would like to take this opportunity to thank CHINFO's Cdr John Fleming, Lt Cdr Danny Hernandez and Lt(jg) David Luckett for handling my request so swiftly, and COMNAVAIRLANT's Deputy Public Affairs Officer Mike Maus for providing me with a base escort 'in the field' at NAS Oceana.

Thank you also to my old friend and fellow naval aviation stalwart Cdr Peter Mersky, whose generous hospitality during my trip to NAS Oceana was most welcome. I also owe my sincere thanks to Capt Anthony Gaiani (CO of VF-213 in OIF), Cdr Sean Clark, Cdr Andy Lewis and Lt Cdr Bobby Baker who painstakingly read through the finished manuscript to ensure its accuracy from the end user's perspective. They also contributed several riveting combat accounts for this book too. Thanks to Christopher J Madden, Director Navy Visual News Service, who supplied examples of his staff's OIF imagery. Photographers Dave Brown, Troy Quigley (VFA-201) and Ray Arnold (VFA-201) also made important contributions. Timely information was provided by Capt Zip Rausa of the Association of Naval Aviation, Capts Steve Millikin and Jan Jacobs of the Tailhook Association, Peter Foster, Peter Quinn, Lt Col Mark Hasara, David Isby and Bob Sanchez.

Finally, thanks to the pilots from the following units whose OIF experiences and photographs fill this volume;

CVW-3 – Capt Pat Rainey
CVW-8 – Capt David Newland and Lt Cdr Matt Pothier
VFA-15 – Cdr Andy Lewis, Cdr Ed Langford, Lt Cdr Norman Metzger and Lt Jon Biehl
VFA-37 – Cdr Michael Saunders and Lt Brian Emme
VFA-87 – Cdr Greg Fenton
VFA-105 – Cdr Tom Lalor, Lt Cdr Bradford Blackwelder, Lt Bobby Baker, Lt Mike Kraus,
  Lt Chris Rappin and Lt Johnnie Caldwell
VFA-201 – Cdr Sean Clark and Lt Cdr Mark Brazelton

Tony Holmes, Sevenoaks, Kent, August 2005

PRELUDE TO WAR

The campaign fought by the Mediterranean-based Hornet units in OIF contrasted markedly with the war that was waged by light strike squadrons flying from aircraft carriers sailing in the crowded waters of the Northern Arabian Gulf (NAG). Although the units from CVW-3, embarked in *Harry S Truman*, and CVW-8, aboard *Theodore Roosevelt*, had started the campaign in a similar fashion to their NAG-based brethren by attacking fixed targets as part of 'Shock and Awe', they soon switched to Close Air Support (CAS) missions for Special Operations Forces (SOF) scattered across northern Iraq.

Both air wings had originally been tasked with supporting the US Army's invasion of Iraq from Turkey, the US government having planned on committing 65,000 troops – including the entire 4th Infantry Division (ID) – backed by 225 combat aircraft and 65 helicopters, to fighting the war on the northern front. This deployment had proved deeply unpopular in Turkey, however, and despite extreme pressure exerted by the Bush administration – and the offer of $30 billion in loans and aid – the Turkish government voted against granting basing rights to US forces on 1 March 2003.

Pentagon war planners quickly shifted the emphasis of the Navy's TACAIR assets in the Mediterranean away from traditional CAS and refocused it on the support of small SOF teams whose job it was to keep the Iraqi Army's IZ Corps occupied while Coalition forces raced for Baghdad from the south.

Relying heavily on the tactics developed during OEF, when again naval aviation was called on to support SOF squads operating in isolation in the rugged wilds of Afghanistan, the Hornet pilots braved enemy AAA and SAMs and endured truly awful weather conditions to ensure 24-hour CAS support for Coalition forces in OIF.

The unfamiliarity of the terrain in northern Iraq also posed a significant challenge for the light strike pilots in OIF. For over a decade naval aviators had been exclusively tasked with performing Operation *Southern Watch* (OSW) patrols, and this meant that the NAG-based

VFA-87's Lot XIII F/A-18C BuNo 164252 comes under tension on CVN-71's bow catapult two on 9 January 2003 during CVW-8's CompTUEx off Puerto Rico. 'Party 412' was still marked with seven bomb symbols and *OPERATION ENDURING FREEDOM* titling beneath its leading edge extension (LERX) when this photograph was taken, although it had been removed by the time 'TR' arrived in the eastern Mediterranean in mid February. During OIF VFA-87 adorned its aircraft with tomahawk symbols for every mission in which its jets dropped ordnance, and BuNo 164252 returned to its home base of NAS Oceana marked up with five tomahawks applied neatly beneath an OIF banner (*PH2 Angela Virnig*)

units were thoroughly familiar with their target sets, the integrated air defence systems (IADS) in southern Iraq and the weather conditions. This was far from the case in the north, where USAF units had dominated Operation *Northern Watch* (ONW) since United Nations' Security Council resolutions 678, 687 and 688 had been put in place in late 1991 to restrict aggressive behaviour by the Iraqi Air Force (IrAF) and Army north of the 36th parallel.

ONW had grown out of Operation *Provide Comfort I/II*, which had in turn been instigated by US forces in the immediate aftermath of Operation *Desert Storm* in March 1991. *Provide Comfort* saw USAF, British and French fast jets (the latter subsequently withdrawn) conducting combat air patrols over a safe haven/security zone created for Kurdish refugees in northern Iraq. Elements of US European Command's USAF-led Combined Task Force (CTF) were primarily based at the US-built air base at Incirlik, near the Turkish city of Adana. Initially charged with securing the airspace in the area for a large-scale air-dropped humanitarian effort in 1991-92, CTF reconnoitred Iraq north of the 36th parallel in order to detect any potential IrAF intervention.

These overflights were vigorously contested by the Iraqis, who were banned from flying fixed-wing aircraft north of the 36th parallel. As with OSW, resistance to CTF overflights usually took the form of AAA and SAMs, and the launch sites and flak batteries were in turn targeted by patrolling Coalition aircraft. The latter usually consisted of USAF F-15Es and F-16CJs, Marine Corps and Navy EA-6Bs (expeditionary units only) and RAF Tornado GR 1s, Harrier GR 7s and Jaguar GR 1s.

Due to the land-locked nature of ONW, sea-based US Navy Tomcats, Hornets and Prowlers were never committed to this mission. Hence, on the eve of OIF, the F/A-18 units of CVW-3 and -8 were busily studying USAF-generated target sets and IADS intelligence information pertaining to northern Iraq.

CVW-3's WORK-UPS

Backtracking a little to the autumn of 2002, CVW-3 was in the final stages of its 18-month-long work-up cycle, which had progressed along normal lines following the completion of its eventful maiden cruise aboard CVN-75 in 2000-01. Air wing staff officers had kept a weather eye on developments in the Middle East, with the Bush administration's case for war against Iraq gaining momentum as discussions about the country's alleged development and stockpiling of weapons of mass destruction reached fever pitch.

Links between Saddam's regime and Osama Bin Laden's al-Qaeda network were also being played up by the White House, and the end result of all this talk was the decision, in September 2002, by US Defence Secretary Donald Rumsfeld to step up the level of response to Iraqi threats to US and British aircraft conducting OSW/ONW missions.

CVW-3 had seen considerable action when last in the NAG in early 2001. Indeed, on 16 February that year, the air wing's aircraft had participated in the largest strike on targets in southern Iraq since Operation *Desert Fox* of December 1998. Either side of the 16th, CVW-3's Hornets had also flown Response Option (RO) strikes against Iraqi radar command, control and communication nodes and AAA sites.

Now it seemed that the air wing would be well placed to take the fight to Saddam Hussein on a broader front.

When CVW-3 got together for its air wing Fallon detachment in early October 2002, its light strike pilots were fully aware that they were conducting their final work-ups in preparation for a war cruise. The situation in Iraq had not improved since the air wing's VFA-37 and VFA-105 (and the Marine Corps' F/A-18A+-equipped VMFA-115, whose OIF action is detailed in *Osprey Combat Aircraft 56 – US Marine and RAAF Hornet Units of Operation Iraqi Freedom*) had completed the air-to-ground phase of their Strike Fighter Advanced Readiness Program (SFARP) some weeks earlier at NAS Fallon, Nevada. The light strike pilots now began to steel themselves for what lay ahead. VFA-105's Maintenance Officer, Lt Cdr Bradford Blackwelder, recalled;

'We knew that something was coming, and we became more demanding in respect to the operational capabilities of our jets during our final training hops at Fallon. In a normal peacetime environment, we would sometimes take a jet airborne with a degraded system that we perhaps would not need for the flight. We can live with a jet that has a weak radar or a poor FLIR in peacetime, for example, but during our air wing Fallon work-up we really pressed the maintainers to get everything functioning as well as they could, as we knew that this kind of effort was going to be required on cruise.

'In the end you have to take what you are given to do the job, but the maintainers stepped up a level with serviceability and the jets performed tremendously for us. This reliability continued once we were deployed, and we did not miss a single combat mission through unserviceability.

'We tailored all of our training pre-war towards defeating the SAM and AAA threats that we had identified as being the most dangerous to us in northern Iraq. We trained hard at Fallon in the techniques that we had developed to defeat the Iraqi IADS. However, there are so many different types of SAMs out there, so many threat aircraft and so many weapons and systems that we can use to defeat them that we chose to focus on the weapons and jets that we thought would pose the greatest threat to us in VFA-105 over Iraq. We decided not to think about the lesser threats, instead concentrating on the IADS we knew that they had.'

Fellow VFA-105 pilot Lt Mike Kraus explained how the unit applied the same kind of focused approach when it came to choosing the weapons it would employ in OIF;

'The Hornet can bring all manner of dumb and smart bombs, J-weapons and missiles to the party, but we made a decision to train on those that we knew would be used for real over Iraq. We therefore made sure that every pilot was fully conversant with their employment.

'It is hard to effectively train the best way to defeat IADS at squadron level, but at least we all had "the numbers in our head" pre-war for the Hornet's systems that we thought would be the most valuable. Thanks to our squadron-level training, we all became thoroughly familiar with the key defensive systems in our jet.

'We had two pilots on the squadron who had just come back from completing the latest Naval Strike and Air Warfare Center (NSAWC) anti-IADS schools, and they developed a training programme that got into all the "beeps and squeaks" of the electronic warfare systems that we

Aside from being VFA-105's maintenance officer during CVW-3's OIF cruise, Lt Cdr Bradford Blackwelder was also kept busy helping his fellow 'Gunslingers' get back aboard CVN-75 as one of the unit's Landing Signals Officers. Having previously served with VFA-195 in Japan, Blackwelder joined the NAS Fallon-based Naval Strike and Air Warfare Center as an instructor following his war cruise with VFA-105 (*Cdr Tom Lalor*)

employ in combat. Thanks to their training syllabus, the unit's overall level of knowledge was significantly increased. Whereas on previous cruises, where I knew enough about certain systems to employ them effectively but did not know all the ins and outs, this time I knew everything there was to know about the equipment we had chosen to use in OIF.'

Despite NSAWC priding itself with providing the most realistic training environment possible for the squadrons that regularly cycle through Fallon, the static nature of the various threats scattered across its weapons ranges did not offer the best preparation for TACAIR crews heading for combat in northern Iraq, as Lt Cdr Blackwelder recalled;

'The Fallon training proved valuable to a point pre-OIF, although the targets on the ranges did not really move. The dummy airfield is always in the same place, and although NSAWC might add a new target or a mobile SAM site here or there, for the experienced campaigner who has been through the place innumerable times before, you know where to look in order to lock up the target before you bomb it. It was just not like that in northern Iraq during OIF.

'Despite the level of our technology, and the improvement in our training post-OEF, it is always going to be hard to pick out enemy soldiers driving down a road in a civilian pick-up truck when there are other vehicles being driven by non-combatants nearby. Such tactics won't allow the enemy to win a war, but it will mean that these types of targets have to be dealt with by soldiers on the ground, rather than by TACAIR.'

Following the successful completion of CVN-75's Joint Task Force Exercise off the Virginia and North Carolina coasts in early November, CVW-3 flew aboard *Harry S Truman* on 5 December 2002 for the Joint Task Group 03-01 six-month deployment to the Mediterranean.

CVW-3 took full opportunity of working with foreign air forces once east of Gibraltar, and Greek F-4s and F-16s were amongst the first fast jet types to 'mix it' with the air wing's F-14s and F/A-18s. Naval aviators also conducted vital bombing practice during Operation *Joint Forge*, which saw them attacking ranges in Albania, Greece, Bosnia and Turkey, often

Watched over by an impressive President Harry S Truman-inspired mural on CVN-75's hangar bay fire/blast doors, VFA-37's CAG jet (Lot XVIII F/A-18C BuNo 165181) undergoes routine maintenance during the vessel's Joint Task Force Exercise off Virginia in November 2002. Behind it are three of VMFA-115's twelve F/A-18A+s, this unit sharing CVW-3's light strike workload with VFA-37 and VFA-105 during OIF (*Cdr Tom Lalor*)

Armed with single live Mk 20 Mod 3 Rockeye II cluster bomb units under each wing and an active AIM-9M missile on its port wingtip rail, 'Canyon 403' (Lot XIII F/A-18C BuNo 164243) heads for an east coast bombing range in November 2002 during CVW-3's CompTUEX. Packed with 247 Mk 118 Mod 0 bomblets, the Rockeye CBU ultimately proved to be one of the few weapons not used by CTF-60 in OIF. BuNo 164243 ended the campaign with nine bomb symbols adorning its nose (*Lt Bobby Baker*)

in conjunction with SOF FAC teams – this training would subsequently pay dividends in OIF. Hornet crews used the ranges to hone their skills in designating for laser-guided bombs, as such training cannot be conducted effectively at sea. Operating over land proved to be an unfamiliar experience for the pilots, who had been bombing towed targets at sea since leaving home, as Lt Cdr Blackwelder recalled;

'In the final weeks leading up to OIF, we were flying up to 18 sorties per day, only two to four of which would see jets heading over land to bomb ranges in Turkey. We primarily attacked a series of targets at sea, crews briefing to bomb a designated spot in the water. We would launch and then proceed to our target, and once we had completed our bombing we would transition to an air-to-air mission, before returning to the boat.'

Following a brief visit to the Slovenian port of Koper in early February 2003, *Truman* headed for the eastern Mediterranean in preparation for OIF. Whilst en route to its operating area off the coast of Turkey, CVW-3's fast jet crews 'fought' French Super Etendards and Rafales from the carrier *Charles de Gaulle*. Within days of CVN-75's arrival on station it was joined by *Theodore Roosevelt*, with CVW-8 embarked.

CVW-8's WORK-UPS

When CVN-71 sailed into the eastern Mediterranean on 17 February 2003, it marked the culmination of one of the most accelerated carrier work-ups ever undertaken by the US Navy in peacetime. Having played

CVN-75 continues to conduct cyclic ops whilst taking on jet fuel from Military Sea Lift Command's *Supply* class fast combat support ship USS *Arctic* (T-AOE 8) in the Mediterranean. Although the carrier itself is nuclear-powered, and therefore has no need for fossil fuels, the JP-5 reserves for the 60+ aircraft embarked in CVN-75 required regular replenishment every few days during the increased op tempo of OIF. Displacing almost 52,000 tons when full, and designed to provide fuel, provisions and munitions for carrier task groups operating in forward areas, *Arctic* is an impressive vessel in its own right (*PH2 John Beeman*)

The 'T-AOE of the skies', a 173rd Air Refueling Squadron KC-135R of the Nebraska Air National Guard provides JP-5 at 25,000 ft during CVW-8's CompTUEx in January 2003. All three F/A-18Cs are equipped with orange AN/ASQ-40T large area training range pods on their wingtips (*Lt(jg) Rob McClure*)

VFA-87's 'Party 406' (Lot XIV F/A-18C BuNo 164644) is guided onto the launch shuttle of bow cat two during cyclic ops in the eastern Mediterranean on 26 February 2003. Prevented from using bombing ranges ashore, CVW-8's trio of Hornet units were restricted to attacking 'splash targets' off Cyprus in the weeks prior to OIF. VFA-87 had, however, been given the chance to expend plenty of ordnance during the CompTUEx that immediately preceded the combat deployment, 'War Party' jets firing several air-to-air missiles and dropping more than 300 bombs (a mixed bag of LGBs, Mk 82/83/84 general purpose and inert Mk 76 practice bombs) on the Vieques range. Delivered new to VFA-87 in January 1992, this aircraft ended its OIF deployment adorned with ten 'tomahawk' bomb symbols (*PH3 Matthew Bash*)

a major role in OEF in 2001-02, which included a record-breaking 159-day line period in the northern Arabian Sea, *Theodore Roosevelt's* original work-up cycle had called for the carrier to deploy, with CVW-8 embarked (in place of CVW-1), in May 2003. However, once Commander Naval Air Force US Atlantic Fleet received word from the Pentagon in August 2002 that the White House's stance on Iraq was hardening, CVN-71 and CVW-8 were instructed to accelerate their work-ups.

Capt David Newland was the man responsible for overseeing CVW-8's hasty turnaround, the CAG explaining just how this was done;

'Normally, an air wing gets three weeks with NSAWC at Fallon, but we got just 15 days. Our work-up was mixed up due to "TR" coming out of the navy yard so late in November. This meant that we actually went to Fallon *prior* to doing our carrier quals on the ship the following month.

'Our Composite Training Unit Exercise (CompTUEx) was brought forward ten days to 6 January 2003, after which we headed down to the Puerto Rican operating areas and got our bombing certifications and were then told to immediately deploy to the Mediterranean. Although we knew when we left Norfolk in early January for the CompTUEx that there was a chance we were not going to come back following the completion of our training, it was still a little traumatic for the crew to be told that we were deploying straight away. However, we knew that something was brewing, and we were told that we had to be in the eastern Mediterranean, ready for combat operations, by 17 February.

'It would have been a huge challenge for us had we actually gone to war on that date, for we had really run down our stocks of parts and ordnance during the accelerated CompTUEx.'

CVW-8's permanently assigned light strike units – VFA-15 and VFA-87 – proved up to the challenge presented by the accelerated work-up cycle, the latter unit flying an astounding 252 sorties in less than 15 days during its air wing Fallon training. VFA-15's pre-cruise preparations were overseen by its CO, Cdr Andy Lewis, who had flown A-7E Corsair IIs during *Desert Storm* some 12 years earlier;

'I had initially joined VFA-15 as its Executive Officer just as the unit was deploying for the Mediterranean in April 2001 for what promised to be a fun-filled trip of several port visits and some great flying. After our obligatory time in the NAG doing OSW missions during July and August, we were diverted from our planned port visit to Cape Town, in South Africa, when the events of 11 September occurred. Having subsequently taken part in the first actions of OEF, we returned from that deployment in mid-November 2001 to a changed America.

'After going through the first part of a "standard" turnaround, I took command of VFA-15 in August 2002. We started our formal preparation

for deployment the next month with our first trip to NAS Fallon for the air-to-ground SFARP. At that point, we were pretty sure of a few things. Firstly, the likelihood of taking offensive action in Iraq was increasing with each day. We were scheduled to deploy in May 2003, but I was certain that it would be right after our last at-sea work-up in January.

'Secondly, I was certain that the mundane aspects of rendezvousing with and refuelling from "big wing" tankers were going to be the real challenges of any strike operations that we took on. Additionally, the AN/AAS-38A NITE Hawk FLIR pod in the F/A-18 was not the greatest piece of "kit", and we needed to train doubly hard as LGBs were becoming the weapon of choice until the 1000-lb JDAM came on line.

'Thirdly, we had six "nugget" pilots in the squadron. All of the youngsters were pretty talented, but we needed to get them up to speed a little sooner than I had originally thought.

'Fourthly, CVW-8 had a different composition than for its previous deployment. We went from two F-14 and two F/A-18 squadrons to a single Tomcat unit and three Hornet squadrons. This was more or less a normal air wing configuration for the period, with the exception that one of our Hornet squadrons was VFA-201 – a mobilised Navy Reserve squadron from NAS/JRB Fort Worth, Texas. The wealth of experience that the reservists brought to the air wing was good, but they did not join until November 2002, and their jets and people had lots of work to do to get ready to deploy.

'As expected, we departed Virginia in January 2003 and headed for the Mediterranean. The first couple of months of the deployment were spent planning, speculating and trying to train.

'We had access to the Air Tasking Order (ATO) for the first 48 hours of OIF, so the CAG assigned leads for the several strikes that were CVW-8's responsibility. This allowed the air wing to have its mission plans worked out some weeks prior to the commencement of hostilities.

'The only issue relating to these mission that continued to vex us in the lead up to war centred on which route of flight we were going to use. Were we going to fly from the Red Sea or the eastern Mediterranean through western Saudi Arabia, or, as was looking more likely, over Turkey and into northern Iraq? Regardless of scenario, tankers were in short supply.

VF-213's F-14D BuNo 159629 and Lot XIV F/A-18C BuNo 164687 of VFA-87 are seen here just seconds away from launching off the waist cats on CVN-71 during the vessel's transit across the Atlantic in early February 2003. Although Tomcat units assigned to the other air wings involved in OIF regularly conducted buddy-lasing and FAC(A) for Hornet units, VF-213 did very little of this for CVW-8's light strike squadrons because it operated almost exclusively at night. 'War Party 400' was decorated with an impressive 26 'tomahawks' by the end of OIF, this tally being beaten only by 'Party 403' with 31 (*PHAN Aaron Burden*)

The pilot of VFA-201's 'Hunter 211' (Lot IX F/A-18A+ BuNo 163113) has extended his tailhook as he returns to the marshall overhead CVN-71. Delivered to the Navy in January 1987, this jet was VFA-201's 'warhorse' in OIF, as it flew the most combat missions (24) and stayed on the flightdeck in an up status for the entire aerial campaign (*Lt Cdr Mark Brazelton*)

VFA-201 was led by Cdr Tom Marotta during OIF. The boss is seen here conducting his cockpit preflight checks (*Ray Arnold*)

'We tried, unsuccessfully, to get access to some overland targets in the eastern Mediterranean, so our training consisted of pretty restricted operations near Cyprus. One thing that we did in our squadron that I think paid big dividends when OIF started was to create a tactical organisation, or, in other words, assign permanent lead-wingman combinations. We took the most experienced pilots and paired them with the least experienced. After that, pilots were assigned by tactical pair as strike sorties were given to the squadron. As a result, my young guys were never without guidance either before or during the war, and this allowed even the most junior "nugget" to fly strikes starting from day one, regardless of their overall experience.'

MOBILISATION

As Cdr Lewis previously mentioned, a third of CVW-8's light strike force consisted of a dozen F/A-18A+s flown by Reserve-manned VFA-201 'Hunters'. The Texas-based unit made history in 2002-03 when it became the first tactical Reserve squadron to be mobilised and deployed since the Korean War, some 53 years earlier. VFA-201 was manned by a cadre of very experienced naval aviators, including Cdr Sean Clark, who wrote about his squadron's call to arms in *The Hook*'s Summer 2003 issue;

'Word that a Reserve VFA squadron might be mobilised spread through the command during the July 2002 drill weekend. In fact Cdr Tom Marotta, VFA-201 CO, was asked by his boss, CAG CVWR-20 Capt Stan O'Connor, to determine how many sailors from his command would volunteer for mobilisation if the air wing were to assemble personnel and aircraft collected from the air wing's squadrons. It was immediately apparent from the poll that VFA-201 wanted no part of being chopped up and sent to a "made up" unit of volunteers. To a man, the squadron declared it was "all for one and one for all" – the "Hunters" were more than willing to go as a squadron if mobilised. Marotta would later recall that it was one of the proudest moments of his command tour.

'With the rumours of mobilisation still buzzing, the squadron continued to train with the Army's forward air controllers from Fort Hood and Fort Sill. The "Hunters" even began flying more Night Vision Goggles (NVG) sorties to sharpen up their night strike capabilities.

By September, and the annual CVWR-20 detachment, VFA-201 was ready for the two-week det to NAF El Centro, where it claimed the air wing bombing trophy. The unit also returned from the detachment with its marching orders in hand.

'While the squadron was flying in El Centro, CAG O'Connor had meetings in San Diego with Commander Naval Air Forces Pacific

Fleet concerning the mobilisation of VFA-201 – war loomed in Iraq and the Super Hornet transition was progressing at a less-than-optimum pace. The latter was creating a hole in CVW-9, which forced the Navy to look at other options to complete an air wing. O'Connor pointed out that the "Hunters" were ready, and would not disappoint.

'The mobilisation was to require some monumental achievements in order to succeed. One included transferring our 12 unmodified A-model jets to sister squadron VFA-203 and accepting 12 F/A-18A+s from VFA-203 and -204 in return. The latter version of the Hornet is a more advanced jet compatible in all respects with the Navy's newest weapons systems as employed by the F/A-18C and the F/A-18E/F.

'Marotta asked all personnel to be ready to mobilise on 30 September, as senior Pentagon leaders were to decide the squadron's fate later that week. While VFA-201's maintenance troops worked feverishly to ready the aircraft, squadron pilots had arranged for specialised training on the unfamiliar sensors and weapons systems in the "new" aircraft.

'Marotta soon received orders from CAG O'Connor telling him that VFA-22, recently assigned to CVW-8 from CVW-11, was to fill the CVW-9 spot instead. But O'Connor also said that while the hole in CVW-9 had been filled, it created yet another in CVW-8. He advised the skipper that VFA-201 might be used there instead. Sure enough, on 5 October the unit received formal mobilisation orders instructing it to join CVW-8.

'The squadron's first week on active duty was filled with briefings and lectures. VFA-201 would also have to complete an accelerated SFARP syllabus in just three weeks, prior to meeting its new air wing at Fallon in November.

'With the help of the Atlantic Fleet Strike Fighter Weapons School, the "Hunters" received updates on the latest tactics, weapons and threats in preparation for a nine-sortie flight syllabus the following week. The squadron would fly those sorties in the Dallas/ Fort Worth area, which meant

Wearing freshly applied markings, 'Hunter 200' (Lot VIII F/A-18A+ BuNo 162904) is seen carrying three not so pristine 330-US gal external tanks – a rare fit except when transitting between bases or out to the ship. The fighter's section lead carries an AIM-9M captive training round on its starboard wingtip rail. Delivered to the Navy in October 1986, this aircraft was subsequently issued to VFA-151 as the Japan-based unit transitioned from the F-4S to the F/A-18A. A veteran of *Desert Storm*, the jet returned to CONUS in mid 1991 when VFA-151 replaced its A-models with F/A-18Cs. Assigned to Reserve-manned VFA-203 at NAS Cecil Field, Florida, in 1996, the fighter was one of around 200 A-models upgraded to A+ standard in 2001-02. It was passed on to VFA-201 in the autumn of 2002 (*Lt Cdr M Brazelton*)

'Hunter 200' is marshalled towards a catapult during CompTUEx (*PH3 Phillip Nickerson Jr*)

that the squadron's maintainers could continue accepting F/A-18A+s without any significant interruptions.

'Passing SFARP with the highest marks given that year to any F/A-18 unit, VFA-201 then headed off to Fallon for three weeks of planning and flying large scale air wing strikes. Lessons learned here would later prove helpful as the "Hunters" prepared for war. Following the success of Fallon, VFA-201 began preparations for more work-ups and carrier qualifications. To achieve the latter, more than a thousand day and night practice carrier landings were carried out at NAS/JRB Fort Worth over a three-week period. In typical Texas fashion, the good citizens of Fort Worth were seen lining the fence daily to cheer the squadron.

'VFA-201 then flew to the unit's newest home, *Theodore Roosevelt*, for carrier qualification and cyclic operations. Again performing flawlessly, the squadron qualified all 18 of its pilots in day and night carrier operations while earning CVW-8's highest landing grades. This was especially noteworthy, seeing that some of the squadron's pilots had not been to the carrier at night in more than 13 years!

'From the outset, it was apparent that the "Hunters" would be tough to beat around the boat – the average pilot was 35 years old, had 350 carrier landings and 2700 flight hours under his belt, and 14 of the 18 were graduates of the Navy Fighter Weapons School (TOPGUN).

'After a brief period at home for Christmas, squadron personnel were told to pack their bags, as it was likely that they would not be back after the upcoming at-sea period. The "Hunters" completed three weeks of CompTUEx training in the Puerto Rico operations area in January, leading strike sorties in the Vieques target complex. Proving their experience, the Reserve pilots led CVW-8 during its accelerated training schedule in many areas of strike warfare. On 31 January CVN-71 was ordered to proceed to the Mediterranean, taking VFA-201 with it.'

The 'Hunters' were mentored within CVW-8 by VFA-15, as squadron executive officer Cdr Ed Langford explained;

'VFA-15 buddied up with VFA-201 pre-cruise, the pilots coming to our training lectures and the maintenance departments working together. This was primarily because the unit's commander officer, Cdr Tom Marotta, my CO (Cdr Lewis) and I were all winged together at NAS Beeville, Texas, in 1987. Marotta and I also completed our first two fleet deployments together. When we found out that VFA-201 was joining CVW-8, the senior officers from both VFA-15 and -87 met and immediately decided that we had to get together in order to bring the reserve unit up to speed in the quickest possible time.

'To this end, some VFA-201 pilots actually flew our jets to get their carrier qualifications, as their aeroplanes were still having problems with the new software that had been fitted to allow them to operate the latest J-weapons. The software snags initially slowed VFA-201 up in the first weeks of the cruise, but

Armed with an AIM-7M training round attached to an underwing LAU-115 launcher, VFA-15's 'Valion 311' (Lot XIV F/A-18C BuNo 164680) departs CVN-71 via waist cat four during the CompTUEx. Fitting training rounds to aircraft allows groundcrews to practise loading and downloading actual ordnance. It also permits systems interfacing between the aircraft's avionics and those fitted in the weapon itself, as well as exercising the weapon stores' computers. VFA-15 also carried live Sparrow rounds during the CompTUEx, successfully firing three AIM-7Ms against drone targets as part of the exercise (*PH2 Jeremy Hall*)

by OIF these had been completely sorted out, allowing the unit to use the same weaponry that we employed.

'We had known most of the Reserve pilots when they were in the frontline, and they were all experienced hands. The biggest problem they faced was the fact that they had operated almost exclusively as adversary pilots for so long. This meant that they did not routinely practise "blue air", or offensive, mission tactics. However, being very high-time Hornet pilots, they quickly ironed out these tactical wrinkles.'

VFA-15's maintenance officer, Lt Cdr Norman Metzger, outlined the problems facing VFA-201's maintainers in the early stages of the cruise;

'The "Hunters" were only capable of doing what they did because they had the right pilots in the unit, all of whom were vastly experienced. This meant that the aviator aspect of the mobilisation was completely doable. The area where the squadron initially struggled was in the maintenance of its jets during "blue water" ops. The unit had people who had never been to sea before, having spent all their lives on P-3s until they joined the Reserve. These individuals, some of whom were in their mid to late 30s, experienced a really steep learning curve on the maintenance side, and although they were not really ready for a war cruise when we deployed, these guys were not afraid to ask our maintenance people how things worked – and that is how VFA-201 got through the deployment.'

WAR PLANNING

Although both CVN-71 and CVN-75 had arrived on station in the eastern Mediterranean on schedule, exactly how their 140+ aircraft were to be used in OIF was still being

The forward flightdeck area of CVN-71 is crammed with aircraft during a rare break in cyclic ops for CVW-8 during its accelerated CompTUEx. The carrier is almost certainly conducting a Vertical Replenishment at Sea, with the aft deck cleared of jets to allow vital stores and ammunition to be dropped off by CH-46s from the T-AOR sailing alongside the carrier (*Lt Cdr Mark Brazelton*)

CVW-3 DCAG Capt Pat Rainey (seated, pencil in hand) marks up his ingress and egress routes for CTF-60's strike on Saddam Hussein's presidential palace, on the banks of Tharthar Lake. This mission was flown on the morning of 22 March 2003 (*US Navy*)

deliberated following problems securing basing rights in Turkey for US Army troops. One of those involved in the pre-war planning of the northern front campaign was CVW-3's DCAG, Capt Pat Rainey;

'I had joined CVW-3 as DCAG from *Theodore Roosevelt*, where I had been the carrier's Operations Officer during OEF. In the weeks leading up to OIF I was the CVW-3 representative in meetings called by Joint Task Force-Southwest Asia's Combined Air Operations Center (CAOC) at Prince Sultan Air Base ("PSAB"), and I also attended the big DCAG conference in Bahrain, which was chaired by Fifth Fleet commander Vice Adm Timothy Keating. I was then sent to Turkey to discuss airspace issues with the Turkish general staff. Finally, about ten days before OIF, I travelled to US European Command in Stuttgart to work out how best we could integrate CVW-3 with the 4th ID and SOF assets in the north following the start of the war. I effectively spent the first two months of the cruise going to meetings and working up the airspace for Carrier Task Force (CTF) 60 in the Mediterranean.'

One of Capt Rainey's squadron COs was Cdr Tom Lalor, who led VFA-105. He recalled how CVW-3's mission planners had spent many hours working out the best routes to their targets, only to have these sorties unravel when Turkey closed its airspace to Coalition aircraft;

'Flying in OIF from the Mediterranean was a challenge in many ways. As soon as it appeared that Coalition forces might go to war with Iraq, we began planning for the air campaign to be flown from carriers in the eastern Mediterranean to targets in northern and western Iraq. As the crow flies, the shortest distance from the carrier into Iraq was across Israel and Jordan. However, for political reasons, using Israeli airspace to attack Iraq was eliminated as a viable option. We therefore considered a modified route around the very southern tip of Israel, yet still crossing Jordanian airspace. Again, this was ruled out due to political sensitivities.

'The more we examined our choices, the more flying across southeastern Turkey, skirting its border with Syria and then dropping down into Iraq from the north made the most sense. This route became even more attractive when we learned that the 4th ID would invade from Turkey and create a northern flank in the ground campaign.

'As time passed, however, even the Turkish option fell into jeopardy when the Turkish parliament rejected their President's efforts to support the use of its territory as a jumping-off point for Coalition forces tasked with opening up the northern front. This setback not only affected the ground forces, but also closed Turkish airspace as well, thus sealing off our attack route and seemingly keeping CTF-60 out of the fight. It looked to us like we were going to have to watch this one happen "through the fence". We would sit by helplessly as the carriers in the Persian Gulf took the fight to the enemy. It was a frustrating time in mid March.'

This all changed on 20 March when the Saudi government relented in the face of US pressure and agreed to allow Coalition jets to pass through its previously restricted airspace. The Saudis would not, however, allow bombing missions to be launched from bases within its borders.

DCA PATROLS

Two days prior to CVW-3 and CVW-8 conducting their first long range 'Shock and Awe' strike missions of OIF, both air wings flew their first sorties over Iraq when they carried out defensive counter air (DCA) patrols near Al Taqaddum air base. Located only 40 miles due west of Baghdad, Al Taqaddum was deemed to be the most likely location from where IrAF interceptors would launch in opposition to the 'Shock and Awe' strikes by the Mediterranean-based air wings planned for 22 March.

With ONW having officially ended on 17 March in preparation for OIF, these DCA patrols also allowed Coalition forces to keep tabs on IrAF assets, and to prevent the Iraqis from attempting pre-emptive strikes on Kurdish Peshmerga militia forces massing in the extreme north of the country. Supported by the US Army's 10th Special Forces Group teams and 1000 troops from the 173rd Airborne Brigade, the Kurdish fighters would prove critical to the successful outcome of the campaign in the north following the removal of the 4th ID from the fight.

Leading CVW-3's first DCA mission on 20 March was Capt Rainey;

'CVW-3 had an eight-hour Vul (period of vulnerability) window, during which time we had total responsibility for putting a CAP (combat air patrol) in the "centre lane" right over the base. Both CAG and I flew on the first of these missions, the air wing launching two waves of four jets two hours apart. I was part of the first wave, and we were relieved on CAP by the second wave four hours into the tasking. We effectively rotated four on and four off, our four-ship taking the first four-hour slot and CAG's formation (which comprised two F/A-18s and two F-14s from VF-32) carrying out the second. Our jets were armed exclusively for aerial combat on this mission.

'We hoped to entice the IrAF into the air by performing these CAPs in order to attrite its fighter units before OIF commenced. Sadly, we never saw any effort from those guys to fly at all.

'Iraqi airspace was split up into five CAP stations – northern, centre, southern, southeastern and eastern sectors. We were tasked with patrolling the eastern lane. We approached our CAP station by heading down the Sinai Peninsula and then turning left over Saudi Arabia. We hit the Coalition tanker track over western Iraq, topped off our tanks and then flew the final 140 miles to our CAP station. The CAP was close to the tanker track, so this mission presented us with few problems. We were CAPing near Al Asad, some 80 northwest of Al Taqaddum.

'The missions on 20 March were the only dedicated DCA sorties flown by aircraft assigned to CTF-60 during the entire campaign. The four of us on the first CAP realised just how unique this mission was, and we knew that if any IrAF jets did get airborne in response to our overflights, we would be the first ones in position to retaliate. I was clamouring to be in front of CAG in order to beat him to any aerial kill!'

CVW-8's mixed DCA CAP of F-14s and F/A-18s relieved CVW-3 after eight hours over Al Asad, although its crews also saw no action.

With the IrAF being conspicuous by its absence in the skies over Iraq on the very eve of OIF, the CAOC now deemed that enemy airspace was free of any manned, integrated aerial threat. This effectively meant that Tomcats and Hornets which would have been assigned dedicated CAP missions in 'Shock and Awe' could now sortie as swing-role strike-fighters, armed with LGBs and J-weapons, as well as air-to-air missiles.

Prior to the CAP flights being launched from the Mediterranean, the crews aboard both carriers had been told that OIF was to start in 48 hours'

Photographed on 17 March 2003, 'Party 403' (Lot XIV F/A-18C BuNo 164663) and 'Valion 310' (Lot XIV F/A-18C BuNo 164673) prepare to launch on one of CVW-8's very last training flights prior to the commencement of OIF. Veterans of 11 years of frontline service with CVW-8 by 2003, both of these aircraft had previously seen action in OEF in October 2001 (*PH3 Sabrina A Day*)

Equipped with an adversary-marked centreline tank (a hangover from VFA-201's previous life as a dedicated fleet adversary squadron), 'Hunter 211' has been armed with live AIM-120C AMRAAMs and AIM-9Ms. This photo was taken late in the afternoon of 20 March 2003, just as pilots assigned to CVW-8's first DCA mission over Al Taqaddum air base were manning up their jets. With not an LGB or JDAM in sight, VFA-201 sortied four F/A-18A+s in this rarely seen fighter configuration on the eve of OIF. Within 48 hours bombs had permanently replaced air-to-air missiles (*Cdr Sean Clark*)

time. Rear Adm John Stuffle-beem, commander of CTF-60, also informed CVN-75 that it was to operate during daylight hours, while CVN-71 would undertake the night carrier mission. Cdr Clark of VFA-201 explained what impact this had on CVW-8;

'On 20 March the ship switched the clocks to conform to our new night carrier mission, which meant that breakfast was served at 1900 hrs, lunch at midnight and dinner at 0500 hrs. Each pilot reprogrammed his body while planning for the first night's sorties.'

The day/night split was adhered to throughout the OIF campaign, both in the NAG and in the eastern Mediterranean. One of the few problems to arise following the division of missions in this way was explained to the author by Cdr Greg Fenton, Executive Officer of VFA-87 during the OIF cruise;

'We soon found that *Truman* was having problems keeping its crews night current in its role as the day carrier. The two carrier schedules were therefore adjusted so that CVW-3 got some night flying too. That effectively pushed CVW-8's schedule to the right a little bit so that while we were still launching at night, we did get some day recoveries. More importantly though, CVN-75 was able to maintain some of its aviators' night currency. CVW-8 did no pure day strikes where we took off and came back in the day, but for some crews it was daylight by the time they were over Iraq.'

With OIF now just hours away, and Turkish airspace still closed to Coalition aircraft, the naval aviators tasked with flying the first missions from the eastern Mediterranean stared eight- to nine-hour missions squarely in the face. For the pilots of VFA-15 and VFA-87 in particular, who had endured sorties of a similar length during OEF some 18 months earlier, the task that lay ahead of them seemed all too familiar. Nevertheless, TACAIR crews were thankful that the waiting was at last over and 'A-Day' (the commencement of 'Shock and Awe') had arrived.

'SHOCK AND AWE'

For the three carrier task groups sailing in the NAG, the commencement of OPLAN 1003V, as the 'Shock and Awe' phase of OIF was officially referred to in the Pentagon, on 21 March 2003 meant the launching of waves of fighter-bombers bound for targets in and around Baghdad. Their arrival over the Iraqi capital would be preceded by several hundred Tomahawk Land Attack Missiles and Conventional Air-Launched Cruise Missiles, the former having been fired from naval surface and subsurface vessels in both the Mediterranean Sea and Arabian Gulf, and the latter from B-52s. The naval aircraft would be conducting operations in conjunction with USAF fighter and support assets, as well as Royal Air Force and Royal Australian Air Force jets.

Due to the sheer scale of this aerial assault, the best ingress and egress routes to and from the targets assigned to the Fifth Fleet carriers had been pre-planned for weeks in advance, based on intelligence gained from years of OSW overflights of southern Iraq. Tanker tracks had also been worked out months prior to 'A-Day', as had diversionary landing airfields in the event of bad weather or low fuel states. Finally, the CAOC-generated ATO had been set in stone for the first 48 hours of the campaign, this document being issued to the various air wings in early March.

Armed with detailed target information, backed up by good AWACS, EW and tanker support, and in possession of a workable ATO, the naval aviators in the NAG were about as well prepared for 'A-Day' as they could be. The same could not be said of their brethren in CTF-60, however.

The closure of Turkish airspace to all Coalition aircraft in the lead up to OIF had forced the CAOC's mission planners to hastily revise their ATO for 'Shock and Awe'. New routes into northern and western Iraq had to be quickly found, and with only 48 hours to go before the launching of 'A-Day', it appeared as if the aircrews from both CVW-3 and CVW-8 would

Both CTF-60 carriers sailed through some unseasonably poor weather as they departed Op Area One off the coast of Turkey and headed southwest for the Nile Delta just days prior to the commencement of OIF. Shrouded in drizzle, CVN-75 conducts a replenishment at sea with Military Sea Lift Command fleet oiler USNS *John Lenthall* (T-AO 189) about half-a-mile ahead of CVN-71 (*PHAN Chris Thamann*)

be forced to watch the campaign unfolding on CNN, rather than from 30,000 ft over Iraq. This all changed on 20 March, however, as VFA-105's CO, Cdr Tom Lalor, explained;

'Finally, on the day the air campaign began in the south (20 March), we received news that diplomatic efforts to create a Saudi Arabian option had come through. While they would not let any attacks launch from their soil, the Saudi government would allow Coalition aircraft to pass through its airspace. We had a way in! The new route was going to be long. From a position just off the Nile Delta, CVW-3 aircraft flew down the Sinai Peninsula, around the southern tips of Israel and Jordan and worked their way across the Saudi desert to refuel from USAF tankers just short of the Iraqi border. Once topped off, F/A-18s and F-14s, supported by EA-6Bs, would strike at targets located west and northwest of Baghdad.

'As the senior CO in CVW-3, I was tasked by our CAG, Capt Mark Vance, with coordinating the planning of the air campaign from CVN-75. The targets we were assigned were deep in the heart of Iraq. Although initially forced to enter southwest Iraq through Saudi Arabia, we still had to strike targets close to Mosul, Irbil and Kirkuk, in the north. Fuel would be critical.

'We spent countless hours checking and rechecking our figures. Our routes had us coming off target with just a few minutes' worth of fuel available to get to the tanker before we had to divert into an isolated base in western Saudi Arabia. There was precious little margin for error. We spent weeks studying the proper configuration of weapons and external fuel tanks required to strike deep into Iraq with enough firepower to destroy our targets. In the weeks prior to OIF we had conducted "mirror image" strikes that duplicated the speed and distance we would fly. These missions allowed us to check the tanking time required and gave the crews an opportunity to keep their skills fresh for the big day. By the time hostilities commenced, we knew that our plan would work.'

With approval for the Saudi route being given so soon to the start of OIF, a lot of the supporting tanker assets based in Kuwait and Cyprus were either told too late, or not at all, that they had to be in a certain location in order to facilitate the early CTF-60 strikes. This led to some harrowing moments both inbound and outbound from the target, as CVW-3 strike lead, and VF-32 CO, Cdr Marcus Hitchcock explained;

'Nineteen aircraft launched on CTF-60's first OIF mission soon after midnight on 22 March, and we ended up with 13 pressing south to Iraq. The remaining aircraft – four S-3s and two E-2s – did some up front tanking and command and control, before turning back to the ship at a pre-briefed point, leaving the strikers to push into Iraq. It was a very long transit (1400 miles one way) to the target, although we endured this part of the mission a little more comfortably in our Tomcats than our strike brethren did in their Hornets. We got to the Saudi Arabia-Iraq border and rendezvoused with our first "big wing" tankers. The subsequent refuelling session was interesting to say the least, because tankers were showing up at the designated rendezvous point just as we were having to make the decision as to whether to divert jets through a lack of fuel.

'We got to the USAF tankers just in time, but not before losing two Hornets that were timed out before they could refuel – we had a set Vul time that we had to be in Iraq for, and once that was up we had to leave enemy airspace so as not to conflict with follow-up strikes. The tankers were late arriving on station, and it took so long to refuel us that the last two Hornets could not be topped off in time to allow us all to get in and out in our briefed Vul slot. I therefore headed into Iraq with only 11 jets.'

The TACAIR crews duly did spectacular work hitting their targets at Al Taqaddum air base in the early hours of 22 March with 2000-lb JDAM. Both the F/A-18Cs and the F-14Bs delivered three JDAM apiece, all with GPS accuracy, against aim points spread across the large airfield within a matter of seconds. Circling over the target at 30,000 ft, it became readily apparent to a seasoned naval aviator such as Cdr Hitchcock 'that this was a new kind of weapon the likes of which we had never seen before'.

The Joint Direct Attack Munition (JDAM) had become the CAOC's 'weapon of choice' in OSW post-OEF thanks to it being wholly autonomous after release, unlike laser-guided or electro-optical munitions whose accuracy can be affected by bad weather or poor targeting solutions. A clinically accurate weapon against fixed targets, which proliferated in OSW, JDAM is effectively a standard Mk 83 (1000-lb), Mk 84 (2000-lb) or BLU-109 (penetrator) unguided bomb fitted with a GPS guidance control unit (GCU), mid-body ventral strakes and a tail unit that has steerable control fins.

Developed by precision weapons pioneer Boeing in the mid 1990s, the JDAM differs from other GPS-guided weapons such as the AGM-130 and EGBU-15 in that it guides completely autonomously after release – it cannot be steered or fed updated targeting data once dropped.

The 'baseline' JDAM is considered to be a 'near precision' weapon, the bomb's GCU relying on a three-axis Inertial Navigation System (INS) and a GPS receiver to provide its pre-planned or in-flight targeting capability. The INS is a back-up system should the GPS lose satellite reception or be jammed. With GPS guidance at its heart, the JDAM can only be employed by an aircraft fitted with an on-board GPS system so that GPS-computed coordinates can be downloaded to the weapon for both the target itself and the weapon release point. That way the jet's onboard INS remains as accurate as possible while the weapon is acquiring a GPS signal after being released over the target. This effectively means that the jet has to have a MIL-STD 1760 data bus and compatible pylon wiring in order to programme the bomb's aim point, intended trajectory shape and impact geometry.

A VFA-105 pilot conducts his preflight checks on a 1000-lb GBU-35(V)1/B JDAM, fitted with a Mk 83 warhead on 23 March 2003. The JDAM family of precision-guided weapons really came into their own during the war with Iraq, CVW-3's trio of Hornet units expending 78 2000-lb GBU-31s and 216 1000-lb GBU-32/35s. CVW-8's Hornet squadrons dropped 32 GBU-31s (all by VFA-201) and 262 GBU-32/35s
(*PH3 Christopher B Stoltz*)

All of this information will have been loaded by the pilot into his MU (Memory Unit, fitted to the F/A-18C) or MDL (Mission Data Loader, fitted to the F/A-18A+) via the TAMPS (Tactical Aircrew Mission Planning System) pre-flight, should the Hornet be going after a fixed target. If, however, a target of opportunity crops up once in the air, the pilot simply has to enter its coordinates into the Hornet's mission computer and the bomb's aim point is automatically altered.

'Ordies' from VFA-37 use a fuel-powered Single Hoist Ordnance Loading System (SHOLS) to lift a 2000-lb GBU-31(V)2/B JDAM from its Aero-12C skid up to the port wing SUU-63 outer stores station on 21 March 2003 as they prepare aircraft for CVW-3's first OIF strike. Most of the Hornets sortied on the early missions into Iraq carried a hefty bombload of three GBU-31s (*PH1 Michael W Pendergrass*)

A 2000-lb GBU-31(V)2/B, fitted with a BLU-110 warhead, parts company with a VFA-37 Hornet over a cloud-covered northern Iraq. The GPS-guided J-weapons came into their own in conditions such as this, when pilots were unable to achieve a laser lock-on to a target to ensure accurate LGB delivery due to cloud obscuration. Naval aviators had to contend with this kind of weather for much of the northern campaign (*VFA-37*)

Achieving initial operational capability in 1997, JDAM made its frontline debut during the NATO-led bombing campaign in Serbia and Kosovo during Operation *Allied Force* in 1999. It was then progressively employed during OSW, primarily by the US Navy, until the weapon really began to capture headlines during OEF thanks to the exploits of Navy Hornet units operating from the various carriers assigned to the conflict.

As in OSW and then OEF, OIF saw Navy strike units uploading known grid coordinates of static targets into the TAMPS aboard ship, and these were in turn transferred to the Hornet's mission computer via the MU or MDL. Once the target sets had been downloaded, the jet would allocate aim points to each JDAM prior to launch. Employment of the Hornet's radar and NITE Hawk Forward-Looking Infra-Red (FLIR) pod, as well as other external data links and/or secure radio 'comms' from Forward Air Controllers on the ground or in the air, E-2s, E-3s, E-8 J-STARS and RC-135s and RQ-1 Predator or RQ-8 Global Hawk UAVs, allowed the pilot to re-programme his JDAM in flight.

Aside from its stunning accuracy in OSW, OEF and OIF, the weapon also proved popular with crews because it could be released in level flight from high altitude, thus allowing aircraft to stay well above a large percentage of the known SAM or AAA threats. Depending on the height and speed of the delivery platform, JDAM can be released up to 15 miles away from its target in ideal conditions.

DAYLIGHT STRIKE

The first daylight strike by CTF-60 was also made by Hornets, Tomcats and Prowlers from CVW-3, these aircraft having launched at 0400 hrs from CVN-75 while the first wave was still in the air heading back to the carrier. VFA-105's Cdr Tom Lalor played a major part in this mission;

'I was lucky enough to be chosen to lead the first day strike of OIF from the Mediterranean – a 12-jet attack on one of Saddam's palaces on the banks of Tharthar Lake, northwest of Baghdad. Along with the palace, my strike package was tasked with destroying Republican guard barracks in the area now known as the "Sunni Triangle".

'Our CAG, flying with VF-32's CO, had led the first night strike on Al Taqaddum air base just a few hours earlier. Now it was broad daylight, and we did not know how

much of a hornets' nest the first attack had stirred up, as we launched before they had recovered back aboard CVN-75. As with the earlier wave of jets from CVW-3, each of the Hornets and Tomcats in my strike package was loaded with three 2000-lb GBU-31s. This was the largest bomb load I had ever carried in the F/A-18, and the jet flew quite sluggishly on full fuel.

VFA-105's 'Canyon 400' climbs away from 'HST' in afterburner on an atypically clear and sunny day in late March 2003. This aircraft (Lot XIII F/A-18C BuNo 164200) was the unit's most prolific bomber in OIF, bearing 11 LGB, two JDAM and four JSOW symbols on its nose by war's end (*PH1 Michael W Pendergrass*)

'Following the launch, we joined up on an S-3B Viking tanker from VS-22, which would top off our fuel tanks for the long trip to the next refuelling point in northwest Saudi Arabia, where USAF tankers were waiting for us. Because of all the weight hanging off our aircraft, it was tricky manoeuvring the Hornet to get into the refuelling basket at our refuelling speed of 250 knots.

'Once finished, we began the long trek down the Sinai, around the Gulf of Aqaba and up to rendezvous with the three KC-10s flying in trail of each other. Each of us had between 8000 lbs and 10,000 lbs of fuel to take on before our tanks were refilled.

'We were scheduled to be supported by USAF F-16CJ Wild Weasels in the target area, and with a target time fast approaching, we could not afford to have anyone struggling to plug into the refuelling basket. To make matters worse, one of our tankers went "sour" (unable to pass fuel) and we had to split its four F/A-18 receivers between the two remaining "sweet" KC-10s. Fortunately, everyone was on their game, and we got the strike package across the tankers with a few minutes to spare before we pressed on our way down the strike route.

'While each member of the strike was a veteran of many OSW missions, this was different. Saddam's regime would be fighting for its

JDAM to the fore, 'Canyon 400' and '412' top off their tanks soon after launching from CVN-75. VS-22 worked tirelessly providing front and back side fuel for CVW-3's strikers in OIF. Indeed, by the end of the campaign, the unit's eight S-3B Vikings had flown more sorties (478) than any other squadron in the air wing (*Cdr Tom Lalor*)

survival, and we could not see him surrendering without offering up stiff resistance. As we penetrated Iraqi airspace for the first time in OIF, each of us scanned the skies for Iraqi MiGs, SAMs or AAA fire. We continuously checked our missile alert gear for signs that we were being tracked by enemy radar. Surprisingly, it was eerily silent.

'We crossed the southwestern desert of Iraq on our way up to our targets, keenly aware of our surroundings and refusing to let down our guard, lest an unobserved bandit jump the strike package. Baghdad was now just 30 miles to the east of us. Still nothing came.

'As we approached the target area, I checked and rechecked the health of the GPS reception on my three JDAM. I verified repeatedly that the coordinates programmed into the bombs were still correct. I double and triple checked that the bomb arm switch was in the right position. To go through weeks of planning and come hundreds of miles, only to bring my bombs home because had I forgotten to put a switch in the right position, would be a mistake I would regret for the rest of my career.

'Finally we reached the release point, and I pressed the "pickle" (bomb release button). Time stood still as I waited for the bombs to come off, but nothing happened. I couldn't believe my bad luck! Then, after an eternity, came those familiar jolts to the airframe as the Hornet released its 6000 lbs of precision-guided bombs into the sky below. For an instant I remember watching them fall gracefully below my jet, spinning slowly as they went. I then turned my attention to the image of the target displayed on the FLIR screen in the cockpit of my aircraft. Thirty seconds and over six miles of fall later, the six bombs belonging to me and my wingman struck their exact aim points on the palace, scattering marble and gold bathroom fixtures all over western Iraq.

'I looked outside again as the 28 bombs landed, each striking its mark within a car's length of its intended point of impact. Once the weapons detonated, the defences woke up. We could see the sparkles of muzzle flashes around the target area. We were too high and too fast, however, to be overly threatened at that point, and turned back to the south, egressing Iraqi airspace as quickly as we could. We found our tankers waiting for us on the other side of the border, topped up our fuel and made our way back to *Harry S Truman*.

'Once back on deck, I had a confession to make to CAG. With the mission successfully behind me, it was now safe to reveal to the Boss that his senior strike lead, the guy he put in charge of coordinating the overall air campaign from "HST", the same guy he chose to lead the first day mission of the war, had up until now never fired a shot in anger in his almost two decades of naval flying. Lucky for me it had worked out.'

Leading one of the Hornet sections in Cdr Lalor's strike package on 22 March was DCAG Capt Rainey, who recalled;

'CVW-3 launched its second strike some four hours after the first package had departed CVN-75. Our targets were Saddam's Tora Tora Presidential Palace, on the edge of Tharthar Lake, and a Special Republican Guard barracks on the western outskirts of Baghdad. Launching at dawn, we entered Iraqi airspace just as the first strike was coming out. The sun was coming up as we were going in.

'I was somewhat apprehensive on this first strike simply because I did not know how effective the Iraqi IADS would be. We had been thoroughly briefed on their SAM and AAA capabilities, and if the IADS were indeed as formidable as we had estimated them to be in our worst case scenario brief, then I had cause to be anxious. As it turned out, the mission went off without a hitch.

'We encountered AAA as we came in line abreast over the target area. The targets themselves were spread out over an area of 20 miles, the palace being out to the west of Baghdad and the barracks further east. I was on the easternmost edge of the formation as we flew past Baghdad, and I could clearly see the AAA being sporadically fired in our direction.

'The strike package had 60 miles' visibility and there was not a cloud in the sky, so both the target area and the AAA were easily spotted. I could see downtown Baghdad, the lake on which the Tora Tora Palace was situated and the palace itself. The latter was some 60 miles further down range from Al Asad air base, and we headed towards the target via Al Taqaddum. At that point in the mission we were only ten miles from the outskirts of Baghdad. When we came off-target after dropping our bombs, we could actually see the impact points of our weapons on the various palace buildings.

'The strike package headed west out over the lake after delivering its ordnance in order to minimise the jets' exposure to IADS, Cdr Lalor leading us back over Al Asad on our return flight to the carrier.

'I had completed four OSW deployments prior to OIF, and I was using my old charts and kneeboard cards for Iraq on this missions. In all that time, the closest I had come to waging war against Iraq was when I was leading a Hornet squadron on "Ike" just before *Desert Fox* in 1998. We had routinely been up to An Nasiriyah and Al Kut on that cruise, reconnoitring the battlefield, but it was *Enterprise* (with CVW-3 embarked) and *Carl Vinson* (with CVW-11) that came in behind us and actually carried out the strikes on Iraqi military targets.

'Having spent many hours patrolling the flat, desert-like terrain that proliferated in the OSW region of Iraq, I was struck by the green, lush countryside immediately north of Baghdad, as well as the mountainous topography of northern Iraq. Indeed, northeast from the Tigris River up to Iran, it was like flying over Colorado. You went from steep mountains to flat plains that were just gorgeous to look at from 30,000 ft.'

CVW-8 STRIKES

As the designated night air wing, CVW-8 was not committed to 'Shock and Awe' until the evening of 22 March, when it sent a mixed force of Tomcats, Hornets and Prowlers into Iraq to attack targets in Falluja. Refuelling from USAF and RAF tankers en route, the CVW-8 element of the overall strike package then rendezvoused with four USAF F-15Es, four RAF Tornadoes and a pair of F-16CJs in western Iraq.

CVW-8 CO Capt Dave Newland participated in the mission, flying as a RIO in one of the four VF-213 F-14Ds (each armed with three 2000-lb GBU-31(V)2 JDAM apiece) that led six F/A-18s – two from each of the air wing's three strike fighter units – and a solitary EA-6B into combat;

'I did not give myself the mission lead for the first strike as there was so much other administrative "stuff" going on aboard "TR" which required my attention that I wanted someone to be able to focus exclusively on just planning and flying that sortie. I therefore chose the CO of VF-213,

Naval aviators man and start up their aircraft on the flightdeck of CVN-71 on the evening of 22 March 2003 – the first night of action for CVW-8 in OIF. Both of these Hornets ('Valion 305' in the foreground and 'Party 410' behind it) have been armed with three 2000-lb GBU-31s apiece, as well as wingtip-mounted AIM-9Ms and a single AIM-120C on the jets' starboard fuselage station (*PH2 James K McNeil*)

His right hand firmly gripping the launch 'towel rack' and his jet in afterburner, the pilot of 'Valion 310' (Lot XIV F/A-18C BuNo 164673) is just seconds away from riding 'TR's' waist cat four at the start of CVW-8's 22 March strike on targets in Falluja. CVW-8 dropped a total of 23 GBU-31(V)2s on a presidential palace and Republican Guard encampments during this mission, which lasted an astonishing seven-and-a-half hours (*PH2 James K McNeil*)

Cdr Anthony Gaiani, to lead the first mission.

'On our way into Falluja, while we were still sitting off the tankers over Saudi Arabia, waiting to push into Iraq, I was surprised to see SAMs and AAA going off in the distance through my NVGs. The weather was so clear on that first night that you could literally see forever. We pressed in towards the target and more and more stuff was coming up in our direction. At some point on that first leg pushing north from the tanker, it dawned on me that we were heading for the centre of all that SAM and AAA activity! It was time to go to work.

'This first mission was like an Alpha strike of old, with ten Navy jets in formation going after pre-planned, fixed targets – Republican Guard encampments and a presidential palace. We had the GPS coordinates for the targets prior to launching, which meant that we did not even have to see our aim points in order to hit them, although with the weather being so good we locked the camp and the palace up with the FLIR and watched the bombs score a series of direct hits.

'Although we also hit the nearby palace with clinical accuracy, four of the JDAM that the Tomcats dropped turned out to be duds. The FLIR imagery showed the 2000-lb bombs going right through the target, leaving a big entry hole – they were travelling at near-supersonic speed when they hit – but with no resulting explosion. We actually got FLIR imagery of one of the bombs going through the target and coming out the other side, the JDAM bouncing across a road without exploding.

'The AAA was mostly up at our height, the Iraqis relying heavily on their 105 mm guns. Indeed, some of the bursts were over our heads, and we were cruising at 30,000 ft! This was totally different to OEF, where it was all low-altitude AAA and MANPADs, and you felt very comfortable overflying enemy territory at 25,000 ft.'

VFA-15's Lt Cdr Norman Metzger also participated in CVW-8's first strike of 'Shock and Awe', his formation attacking the palace south of the Falluja barracks complex with 2000-lb JDAM;

'Coming off the ship, the tanking with our organic assets on the first night of OIF was colourful to say the least. There were a lot of aeroplanes

flying around in a small chunk of sky trying to get the job done. Indeed, it was so busy that my wingman did not get "front side gas", forcing him to press on to the USAF tanker with less fuel aboard his Hornet than we had anticipated! Once we got down to the Saudi Arabian border with Iraq, we found plenty of gas available from the KC-135s on station. Our timing was such that the sun was coming up as we pressed into Iraq, and we got a little daylight time over the target area.

'Big wing' tankers provided the life blood for naval TACAIR '24/7' during OIF, with CVW-3 furnishing the customers during the day and CVW-8 taking its turn duelling with the basket at night. This particular Hornet is from VFA-15 (*Lt(jg) Jon Biehl*)

'We sat in the jets for seven-and-a-half hours on that first mission, which is a hell of a long time to be strapped into a Hornet – the jet's seat is not designed to be occupied for that period of time! The most challenging aspect of the mission, especially for my "nugget" wingman, was all the tanking that was required to get to and from the target. Getting plugged into the basket proved difficult, as although the weather was clear, there was plenty of turbulence. Most jets on the first mission refuelled four times during the course of the sortie.

'The KC-135 is a challenging jet for us to refuel from, as although its heavy basket (weighing some 250 lbs) is not affected by turbulence as much as the equipment fitted to the S-3, it is not overly large in size, which leaves you with little margin for error. However, once you get the hang of it, the KC-135 is not too bad, as the hose is quite short in comparison with the equipment fitted to other tankers, preventing it from whipping around too much when deployed.

VF-213's F-14D 'Blacklion 106' (BuNo 163893) is marshalled towards waist cat three to partake in a mixed section CAP with VFA-87's 'Party 414' (Lot XIII F/A-18C BuNo 164205). The latter was one of only two Lot XIII jets (the other being BuNo 164252 'Party 412') to serve with VFA-87 in OIF, this aircraft having been delivered new to VFA-131 in October 1990. The Hornet remained with the latter unit until it was transferred to VFA-87 in 2000. The remaining ten 'War Party' F/A-18Cs are all Lot XIV aircraft delivered new to the squadron in 1991-92 (*PH2 James K McNeil*)

'Our individual package commander on this mission was flying an RAF Tornado GR 4, and we also had some shore-based Prowlers with us from Kuwait. There were two other strike packages flying nearby as we entered Iraq. Our package consisted of 12 jets (four Hornets, four Tomcats and four Tornadoes) split up into three four-aircraft divisions, each of which was heading for separate targets. We approached out target from the south, heading north.

'The toughest part of the mission came when we attempted to deliver our ordnance. The Tomcat crews had not dropped JDAM before, and they were having some procedural issues as we neared the release point. I can just imagine what the atmosphere in the cockpits of those jets must

have been like as the crews tried to figure out where the targets were. To make matters worse, we had some winds at height over the palace that had not been anticipated. The VF-213 F-14Ds were supposed to be the first aircraft across the target and our division was due to be the second, but because the Tomcat crews were busy "putting out fires" in the cockpit, they were all over the place trying to get to the correct drop point. This forced us to deconflict, which we did by climbing above them.

'In the short game, we were getting ready for the bombs to come off, with the Tomcats out in front of us in a very loose formation. With the sun coming up, illuminating an overcast in the east, visuals were terrible. Having put our NVGs up because they were ineffective with the rising of the sun, we found it virtually impossible to keep track of all the Tomcats in the lead division, as they had their formation lights switched off, were not in a tight formation and were zigzagging all over the sky!

'By comparison, our division of four Hornets was in a relatively tight formation, looking for any surface-to-air threats – we were not expecting a lot of opposition from the direction that we approached the palace. Luckily, the target area was unobscured, and all four Hornets were 100 per cent successful in hitting the palace with their ordnance – the same could not be said for the Tomcats, as although their JDAM struck the target, half of the bombs failed to detonate!'

The following night CVW-8 launched its second 'Shock and Awe' strike, the mission being led by VFA-15's CO, Cdr Andy Lewis;

'With OIF imminent, and questions regarding our mission routing still to be resolved, CVW-8 was suddenly removed from CAOC's ATO, with the exception of two strikes that would have us launch from the eastern Mediterranean, fly through western Saudi Arabia, skirt the Jordanian border and strike targets in the vicinity of Baghdad. I was assigned to lead the second of these strikes on night two of operations.

'The first mission had gone pretty well, and my strike was assigned yet another Republican Guard barracks and a broadcasting facility in Falluja. I was the strike lead as well as the overall package lead, so I was to coordinate the efforts of our six strike fighters, two Prowlers and a Hawkeye, as well as a similar number of USAF and RAF assets. It was essentially a deconfliction drill with the Air Force assets.

'My strike went more or less as planned, with the exception of some tense moments on the tanker. The weather was superb, formation and weapon delivery went as briefed, we avoided and/or suppressed all of the SAMs and AAA and, most importantly, the weapons fused on target and everyone came home safely. After those first strikes, we could not find a single CVW-8 mission on the ATO, but we were assured by our folks at the Naval Air Liaison Office (NALO) in the CAOC that our assignments were imminent.'

The 'Shock and Awe' missions flown by CVW-3 and CVW-8 via Saudi airspace came to an abrupt halt on the morning of 23 March after the last jets from Cdr Lewis's package had recovered back aboard CVN-71. Thirty-six hours earlier, and just prior to CVW-3 launching its first strike of OIF, Turkish Defence Minister Vecdi Gonul had announced that the skies over his country would be opened for use by Coalition combat aircraft. Cdr Lewis now understood why the ATO was devoid of any further missions for CTF-60 from its location off the Nile Delta;

'Having been assured by the NALO that we would soon be back in the bombing business, sure enough, on the 23rd, we started seeing strikes into northern Iraq through Turkey being assigned to us for the following day. This was a different situation to the one we had faced in "Shock and Awe", as the targets were more fluid. It looked like we were going to be supporting the SOF guys that were operating in the northern part of Iraq.

'Since the Turkish government would not allow US ground forces through their country, there was not a line of friendly troops identified. Consequently, our missions promised to be some form of CAS. The potential for difficulty was greater due to the fact that we were assigned as the "night carrier" and the weather was not particularly good.'

CVW-3's Cdr Lalor also reflected on the decision to move both carriers away from the Nile Delta for operations through Turkey;

'While we were happy to have the shorter route to the target, the navigators of *Harry S Truman* and *Theodore Roosevelt* now had the difficult job of operating two supercarriers crammed into the northeastern-most portion of the Mediterranean in the tiny space between Cyprus, Syria and Turkey. We were so close that the carriers often operated in sight of each other. Having split the day into two twelve-hour shifts, "TR" and CVW-8 flew at night, while "HST" and CVW-3 got the day. We would launch as the sun was breaking the horizon, only to pass our CVW-8 comrades coming off the night shift. We kept this up continuously for three weeks.

'After taking a day to reposition up north, we prepared to shift the focus of our air campaign from one of attacking fixed infrastructure targets such as Republican Guard barracks and command and control sites, to a highly flexible CAS campaign. Our partners were roughly a thousand American, British and Australian SOF troops scattered throughout northern Iraq.'

The change of location for the CTF-60 carriers had not come a moment too soon for air wing staff officers aboard both vessels. They were concerned about the long-term effect that missions like those flown on 22 and 23 March would have on their crews – especially those flying single-seat Hornets – should they have to be sustained for the duration of OIF. One of those 'staffers' was CVW-3's DCAG, Capt Rainey;

'CAG and I thought that the air wing was going to be forced to fly eight- or nine-hour missions as a matter of course. We were left scratching our heads wondering how we were going to generate the number of sorties requested and still keep the days short enough to allow the crews to fly the missions and be able to get sufficient rest to go again the next day. We were very happy, therefore, that the Turks acquiesced soon after OIF stated, allowing us to fly through their airspace. This approval shortened out missions by up to five-and-a-half hours.'

Very few crews had actually been involved in the four strikes flown by CTF-60 on 22/23 March, with VFA-105's Lt Cdr Bradford Blackwelder being one of those to miss out;

'Only four pilots from my squadron had participated in the opening strikes of OIF after CVN-75 had been yanked down south due to the Turkish airspace ban. No tactical jets could have hit targets in northern Iraq from the eastern Mediterranean without tanker support over Turkey, and we initially did not have this. Indeed, only British-based B-52s and P-3s from Crete had the range to reach targets in the north during the first 72 hours of the war. Fortunately, airspace clearance was then worked out, and CVW-3 effectively shut down for 48 hours as the carrier steamed northeast towards the Turkish coast.

'The four guys that were involved in the first missions on 22 March told us that they were more scared by tanking in the gloom than by Iraqi IADS on these strikes. That set the tone for the first ten days of the war once we were up off Turkey, as we had to struggle through bad weather to find the tanker in the first place, and then remain plugged in long enough in cloud to top off our tanks.'

'SHOCK AND AWE' BRIEFLY RESUMES

Arriving on station in Op Area One off the coast of Turkey in the early hours of 24 March, the CTF-60 carriers quickly resumed their strikes on fixed 'Shock and Awe' targets as part of CAOC's hastily revised ATO. CVW-3 managed to launch two waves of strike aircraft in worsening weather against SAM-related targets in Mosul and Tikrit before ending its period as the duty carrier. Capt Rainey, piloting a VMFA-115 F/A-18A+, sortied as part of the second formation;

'My strike package was tasked with attacking a radar relaying facility in the Tikrit area. Everyone in the formation had previously dropped bombs on the 22nd except for my wingman – a department head major from VMFA-115 – and I. As we sat on the tanker replenishing our fuel, we were talking about how northern Iraq looked nothing like we had imagined it would. We were used to the flat OSW landscape, where it was difficult to pick out targets. Instead, here we were tanking right next to Mosul, and you could see the roads, highways and lush green fields.'

CVW-3's Prowlers and Hornets also struck SA-2 and Roland SAM batteries near Kirkuk whilst conducting Suppression of Enemy Air Defences (SEAD) during the course of this mission after the strikers had been lit up by search radars. Several well-placed AGM-88 High-speed Anti-Radiation Missiles soon eradicated the threat, these rounds being amongst the first of 48 HARMs expended by CVW-3 in OIF – 12 were fired by the wing's trio of Hornet squadrons, and the remaining 36 by CVW-3's EA-6B unit, VAQ-130. The AGM-154A Joint Stand-Off Weapon (JSOW) was also a key weapon in the SEAD campaign, both in the NAG and in the north. Lt Cdr Blackwelder explained how his unit employed this GPS-guided bomblet dispenser;

'We dropped a JSOW every three or four days in OIF. Most flights launched from CVN-75 with at least a single Hornet carrying one of these weapons on an underwing pylon. You would make sure that the mission planners knew which aircraft had the JSOW, and where the jet would be operating during the sortie so that a pre-planned target could be located for it. Because of its precision capabilities, the pilot

Raytheon's AGM-154A JSOW proved very effective against the Iraqi IADS threat in the north, particularly in the early stages of the war. Used exclusively by the F/A-18, the intertially-guided, GPS-aided gliding submunition dispenser can be launched up to 35 kilometres away from the target. CVW-8's Hornet units expended 22 JSOW, and although the author was unable to obtain a definitive figure for CVW-3, it would be fair to assume that a similar number were dropped by its trio of Hornet squadrons. In comparison with their NAG-based brethren flying with CTF-50, it would appear that CTF-60 squadrons expended only a third of the number of JSOW dropped by F/A-18 units in the south – CVW-14, for example, got through no fewer than 65 AGM-154s, valued at US$160,000 apiece (*Cdr Tom Lalor*)

carrying the JSOW would usually be told of his target straight after leaving the ship, rather than once the first aerial refuelling had taken place and the flight had pressed south.

'The FAC guys never prescribed targets for the JSOW jet due to the CAOC's insistence that only pre-planned sites could be hit by it. This was because of the nature of the ordnance JSOW carried – anti-personnel bomblets – and CTF-60's desire to avoid civilian casualties at all cost. JSOW was a weapon that the senior brass wanted to know exactly where it was going, so clearance for its use always came from high authority.

'Typically, targets hit with AGM-154As had to have been located and filmed by a Predator UAV, with the resulting imagery then being thoroughly analysed before it was selected for a JSOW attack. These targets could be time sensitive, having just been located, or they might have been on the pre-OIF list for destruction – we were not party to these decisions at squadron level.'

VFA-105's Lt Kraus also explained to the author that HARM was primarily used during the first ten days of the campaign, when CVW-3 was flying a mix of CAS and dedicated strike missions that had been pre-planned. The weapon was rarely used in the direct support of CAS sorties.

When it came to SEAD, CVW-8 led the way in OIF in terms of the number of HARMs it employed against SAMs and Iraqi radar sites. The air wing's trio of Hornet units fired 52 in total, with SEAD specialists VAQ-141 expending a further 22. No other air wing in the NAG or the Mediterranean could match these numbers.

VFA-201's Cdr Sean Clark fired one of the 14 AGM-88s shot off by his unit in OIF – the 'Hunters' launched four HARMS in one mission against active SA-2 and SA-3 sites defending Kirkuk in late March – and he explained to the author how the SEAD mission worked within CTF-60;

'First of all, there were generally a few aircraft (F/A-18s and/or EA-6Bs) assigned to each package that went into country whose sole mission was SEAD support. The Hornets were typically loaded with two AGM-88s and one AGM-154A JSOW or, in the case of the Prowler, just two HARM. Both weapons provide excellent stand-off capability, and were instrumental in clearing the path through readily identified IADS.

'The SEAD package would typically loiter somewhere near the strike elements and await targeting from "offboard sensors". This targeting could come from numerous sources, and was generally "very geo specific" – down to "lat/longs" in most cases. Armed with this intelligence, the SEAD section would coordinate the Time On Target (TOT) with the package's strike leader for the employment of either, or both, options available (JSOW and/or HARM). With TOT in hand, the SEAD section would establish the lane of attack for the strikers and fire/drop multiple munitions to provide cover for them as they entered the threat arena.

'This suppression was generally supplied on an "on call" basis in the northern theatre, with very few pre-planned SEAD missions leaving the CTF-60 carriers in support of the strike packages. We always had SEAD assets available during all CVW-8 Vul windows. This was due to the fact that we were getting called into known threat envelopes throughout the conflict, and we could not always count on the fact that we'd be doing CAS with FACs – independent kill box interdiction and prosecution of Time Sensitive Targets (TSTs) regularly popped up once on station.

The AGM-154A's partner in the SEAD mission was Raytheon's telegraph-pole-sized AGM-88C HARM. This particular example, mounted to the Hornet's standard LAU-118(V)1/A launcher, is carried by an F/A-18A+ from VFA-201. Typically, a single HARM round would be carried under each wing by a SEAD-dedicated Hornet, which would in turn be paired up with a sister-aircraft equipped with two or three JSOW. VFA-201 fired a total of 14 AGM-88Cs in OIF, whilst sister-squadrons VFA-15 and VFA-87 expended 19 each and EA-6B-equipped VAQ-141 22. CVW-3's Hornet units fired just 12 between them, but the air wing's Prowler squadron, VAQ-130, made up for it by reducing Navy stocks by 36! (*Lt Cdr Mark Brazelton*)

Most SEAD assets generally "double cycled" due to their paucity in number, but mission-critical status. They would cover a three- to four-hour Vul window, vice the standard two-hour cycle, using two mid-cycle tanking evolutions.

'I can personally vouch for the success of our dedicated SEAD sections, for on 27 March my wingman and I were "actively" engaged by two separate SA-3 missiles while pushing my strike package towards a known SAM battery and associated SAM radar site near Tikrit. Having coordinated our GBU-31 attack to coincide with the SEAD support offered by two elements of F/A-18s, my wingman and I were fired upon by separate SA-3 sites immediately after employing our JDAM. A sense of terror entered both of our voices at this point in the mission, and this was readily apparent when we reviewed our HUD tapes post-mission.

'Without the need to guide our GPS weapons to their aim points, my wingman and I were able to acquire and defend against two missiles being actively guided towards our aircraft. I called for an immediate break turn, and with the assistance of another section of F/A-18s attacking a target some nine miles to our east who gained a "tally ho" on the missiles coming our way, we broke, defended and watched as the two SA-3s "went stupid" some ten or so seconds into the engagement.

'Following post-brief analysis, it was determined that the subject missile radar facility was most likely destroyed by our SEAD support package mid-way through this engagement sequence. Without this support, myself and/or my wingman may very well have spent the rest of the war in the hands of the Iraqis.

'All of CVW-8's HARM shots were taken at night which had a "blinding effect" on our NVGs if the pilot was not prepared for the launch. Since I had never fired a HARM at night, let alone during daylight, I was caught extremely "off guard" by the intensity of the missile's plume when it left the rail – funny how some things are so obvious "after the fact"! There was also the propensity of others in your strike package to be caught off guard by seeing a HARM in-flight when it was coming over their heads while entering the target area. On more than one occasion strike elements called out that enemy missiles were nearby, only to realise shortly thereafter that those missiles were in fact there for SAM suppression.'

Like VFA-201, VFA-87 also played its part in SEAD support for CVW-8 strikers, the unit leading the way in terms of the number of HARMs (19) and JSOW (ten) it expended whilst performing this mission. The squadron's Executive Officer, Cdr Greg Fenton, recalled;

'We enjoyed great success with JSOW and HARM in the campaign against the enemy's comprehensive SAM threat in the north. Of the two systems, JSOW was our weapon of choice against SAM sites. Pre-war, we thought we had a handle on where all the SAM sites were in northern

Iraq, but of course once OIF had started we realised that the Iraqis had moved the missiles around quite a bit. We therefore needed EW assets in-country locating these sites as soon as they started looking for our aircraft.

'Once a site was located, with JSOW, we could stand off far enough away to prevent them from engaging us with the SAM, but we could in turn neutralise the site with clinical precision. Most of our TSTs were SAM sites located by EW platforms, roving TACAIR jets or SOF FACs.

'TST, which had made its combat debut in OIF with the Navy, allowed us to rapidly deal with most SAM threats encountered in the campaign. A typical TST sortie would see a target of interest pop up and be given a quick release order to allow it to be bombed. Despite the quickening of the approval process, there was still a time delay involved in getting the permission order out to the E-2 controller, who in turn had to relay the target coordinates and description to the SEAD striker. We then had to positively ID the target before we could release the ordnance. All this took time, but our ability to react quickly in opposition to new targets has certainly improved thanks to the implementation of the TST doctrine. We have also been practising our ability to react to TST targeting at Fallon with NSAWC.'

CRUCIAL TANKER SUPPORT

With the carriers' switch to Op Area One, USAF and RAF tanker assets at bases in Cyprus, Crete and Bulgaria were called into action for the very first time. Turkey refused to allow tankers to operate from bases within its borders, thus eliminating around 25 per cent of the sites that Central Command (CENTCOM) had identified pre-war as key locations for its 149 KC-135s, 33 KC-10s, four Tristars and eight VC10Ks.

This ban hit CTF-60 very hard, particularly early on in the war, with seven KC-135s that were scheduled for basing in Turkey having to be moved further west to RAF Akrotiri, on the island of Cyprus, soon after OIF commenced. This boosted the number of KC-135s operating from the base with the 401st Air Expeditionary Wing (AEW) to 30, or 15 per cent of the overall tanker force committed to the campaign.

The USAF's ageing KC-135 tanker force struggled to cope with a conflict the size of OIF, which came hard on the heels of OEF, and its increased operational tempo. The Air National Guard's KC-135E fleet

This photograph was taken by VFA-15 'nugget' pilot Lt(jg) Jon Biehl from the cockpit of his jet at dusk during the first days of OIF. Its main subject is the lead F/A-18C from an accompanying 'War Party' SEAD section, its pilot having activated the wing unfold mechanism, released the brakes and eased open the throttle. Heading for one of the bow catapults, the Hornet is laden down with two AGM-88Cs, two AIM-9Ms and a solitary AIM-120C (*Lt(jg) Jon Biehl*)

was in particularly bad shape, being plagued by corrosion and delays in its modernisation and upgrade programme due to a lack of funding and spare capacity at Boeing's Wichita plant. As a result of these myriad problems, there were 51 fewer KC-135s available for this conflict than for *Desert Storm* 12 years earlier.

CVW-3 worked hard in the early stages of OIF to overcome the tanker shortage, as Capt Rainey explained to the author;

'Our sortie generation rate in the first ten days of OIF was handicapped more by a lack of tankers than anything else. Indeed, we could have flown more sorties if we had had access to more fuel whilst airborne. We identified this problem early on in the war, and it was only partially solved by the movement of a handful of KC-135s from Turkey to the Forward Logistics Operating Base (FLOS) that was hastily established at Akrotiri.

'In order to secure adequate fuel supplies for our jets, CAG Vance set up a "front office" that pulled together senior commanders from ashore and aboard the carrier. CAG Vance represented CTF-60 as the strike commander, while the tanker force's point of contact was Col Cathy C Clothier, who was operational commander of the Akrotiri-based KC-135s. The third member of the "front office" was the FLOS commander, who was a heavy bomb wing B-52 guy brought in from RAF Fairford, in the UK. The final team member was Col Charlie Cleveland, Commander Joint Special Operations Task Force-North (JSOTF-N) SOF for northern Iraq.

'The "front office" effectively became the "shepherd's table" of colonels and captains, and these officers would regularly talk to each other two or three times a day. This set-up greatly improved out relationship with the tanker crews. For example, we would come out of country and tell the tanker that we needed to go back in for ten minutes – could they hang around? They would usually reply in the affirmative, or even offer to drag us down range if we wanted them to.

'As with OEF, we initially flew our OIF missions with the S-3s launching first, followed by the Tomcats. Because of their modest range, the Hornets would launch last and refuel straight away, having the S-3s drag them in-country. However, with the Turkish approval to operate in their airspace, we soon discovered that the missions were so much shorter (400 miles, which we covered in 40 minutes) than in the early stages of "Shock and Awe" that having the S-3s drag you down range did not help the Hornet squadrons at all.

'We eventually settled on sending out two Tomcats and two Hornets to the tanker straight off the boat, after which a second formation of four Hornets and a Prowler would be launched some ten minutes later – all nine jets would be part of the same mission cycle, however. Once refuelled, the Tomcat and Hornet formation would then press on down range, thus avoiding a logjam on the tanker.

'Due to the tight fuel margins in the Hornet, you had to time your arrival on station on the Iraqi border to perfection, for if you checked in too early you would be left waiting for the section in front of you to complete their Vul window before you could head in-country. We stuck to our predicated timeline throughout OIF, with our mission lengths being predicated by gas. Some guys dragged their heels a little bit, but we became adamant in CVW-3 that if you were due on station between 1300

Right
Tanker congestion was a frequent problem encountered by TACAIR assets from CTF-60 throughout the war in the north. Having already refuelled, a section of SEAD-equipped VFA-201 jets (the photographer is strapped into one of them) watch an EA-6B from VAQ-130 replenish its tanks from a KC-10A of the 409th Air Expeditionary Group (AEG), based in Bourgas, Bulgaria. Patiently waiting their turn are two long-legged F-14Bs from VF-32, these aircraft, and the Prowler, belonging to CVW-3 (*Lt Cdr Mark Brazelton*)

The primary tanker wing supplying fuel for CTF-60 in OIF was the Cyprus-based 401st Air Expeditionary Wing (ARW), which controlled a fleet of no fewer than 36 KC-135Rs drawn from numerous regular Air Force, Reserve and Air National Guard units. This particular aircraft was deployed to the Akrotiri FLOS by the RAF Mildenhall-based 100th Air Refueling Wing. Its customers are three thirsty Hornets from CVW-8, returning to CVN-71 soon after dawn following a long range strike. Note that the VFA-201 jet plugged into the wingtip drogue is storeless bar its AIM-9Ms, but the 'War Party' F/A-18Cs behind it are still carrying their AGM-88Cs (*Lt Cdr Mark Brazelton*)

hrs and 1500 hrs, for example, come 1500 hrs you were out of the box no matter what. This was because there were other groups flying in the area ready to replace you in Iraq as per the ATO. And more times than not they had already come in-country and started working with the FACs. This meant that all you were doing by hanging on beyond your allotted time was complicating the picture for them, so you needed to get out.'

OEF veteran Lt Cdr Blackwelder had realised early on in the war cruise that pairing the Hornet's modest range with limited tanker support was going to place a great strain on the light strike pilots flying with CTF-60;

'Prior to OIF starting, the skipper called everyone together in the ready room, and those pilots that had seen sustained combat spoke about their experiences. Several senior guys had fought in *Desert Storm* or *Allied Force*, and they spoke about SAMs. I had been involved in OEF, where getting gas had been the biggest threat to our mission proficiency. I felt this was going to be the case once again in OIF, and sure enough that was how it panned out – certainly for the first ten days at least.

'It did not matter what jet you were flying up north – unless you were in a B-52 – you always needed gas. Gas is always an issue with the Hornet, which makes us proficient at managing it. I therefore think that VFA-105 was a little better prepared for fighting the conflict with minimal gas than other units in CVW-3.'

'BUFFs'

Aside from the CTF-60 Tomcats, Hornets and Prowlers, the only other tactical jets officially assigned to the northern campaign were the 14

B-52Hs based at Fairford with the 457th Air Expeditionary Group. As the war progressed, USAF OA/A-10s, F-15Es and F-16CJs also began 'freelancing' north of Baghdad, but in the early stages of the campaign, the mighty 'BUFFs' were regular companions for the strike aircraft of CTF-60, as CVW-3's Capt Rainey recalled;

'The air war up north was exclusively fought by CVW-3, CVW-8 and the B-52s for much of OIF, and we shared airspace with them throughout the campaign. They would fly through the MEZ with impunity, arcing across Iraq at 38,000 ft. There we were down at 15,000 ft, waiting for the ballistic SAM to come at us through the cloud base. Fortunately, we only saw a few of these at the beginning of the war.

'While we were bumping up to the edge of the SAM and AAA window and beating down the Missile Exclusion Zone (MEZ) with HARMs and J-weapons in order to allow our strikers to hit their targets, the B-52 guys would simply come barrelling across the top of us seemingly without a care in the world. Having spotted their contrails and heard them checking in with their AWACS and FACs, we would duly pass the word amongst our Navy formation – "Okay, standby, here they come" – as they dropped their bombs.

'It took us a little while to work out when to get out of the "BUFFs'" way and when to stay put on station, and that is where pre-mission coordination with the "front office" B-52 guy from Fairford proved crucial. He would tell us what targets they had scheduled, and if they duplicated any that we were attacking according to CVW-3's daily ATO. If the air wing *was* going for the same target, we would say to him, "We can share the target, just as long as you give us a call when you are in-bound. We will then make sure that we are well out of your way."

'After about ten days of butting heads with the B-52 guys, we had worked out how best to operate with them. We soon realised that they weren't too manoeuvrable when on their bombing runs, the B-52 possessing a turning circle the size of northern Iraq. They therefore had to rely on us to give way!'

Both CVW-3 and CVW-8 soon made the shift from attacking fixed 'Shock and Awe' type targets to supporting SOF teams that were rapidly infiltrating Iraq from Kurdish-held territory. The stage was now set for what ultimately proved to be naval aviation's biggest challenge in OIF.

The pilot of 'Bull 307' (Lot XVIII F/A-18C BuNo 165171) is guided onto bow cat two by a yellow-shirted plane director. The catapult crew, in green vests, will spring into action once the jet is in position, the hold-back bar, resting on the left shoulder of the sailor in front of the 'yellow shirt', and the catapult shuttle (the latter is just about to pass between the feet of the plane director) being key elements in the launch process
(*PH1 Michael W Pendergrass*)

COLOUR PLATES

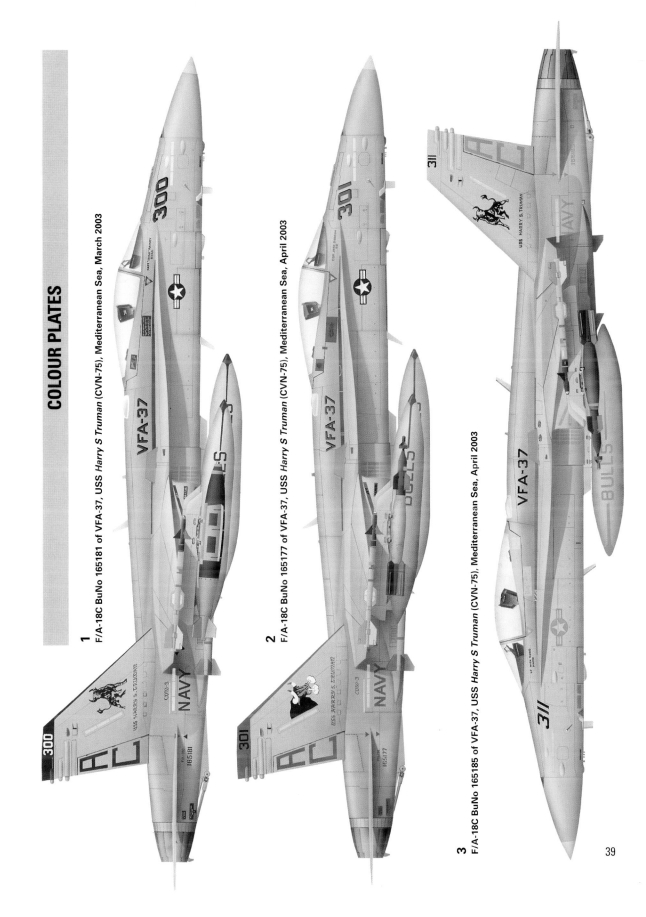

1
F/A-18C BuNo 165181 of VFA-37, USS *Harry S Truman* (CVN-75), Mediterranean Sea, March 2003

2
F/A-18C BuNo 165177 of VFA-37, USS *Harry S Truman* (CVN-75), Mediterranean Sea, April 2003

3
F/A-18C BuNo 165185 of VFA-37, USS *Harry S Truman* (CVN-75), Mediterranean Sea, April 2003

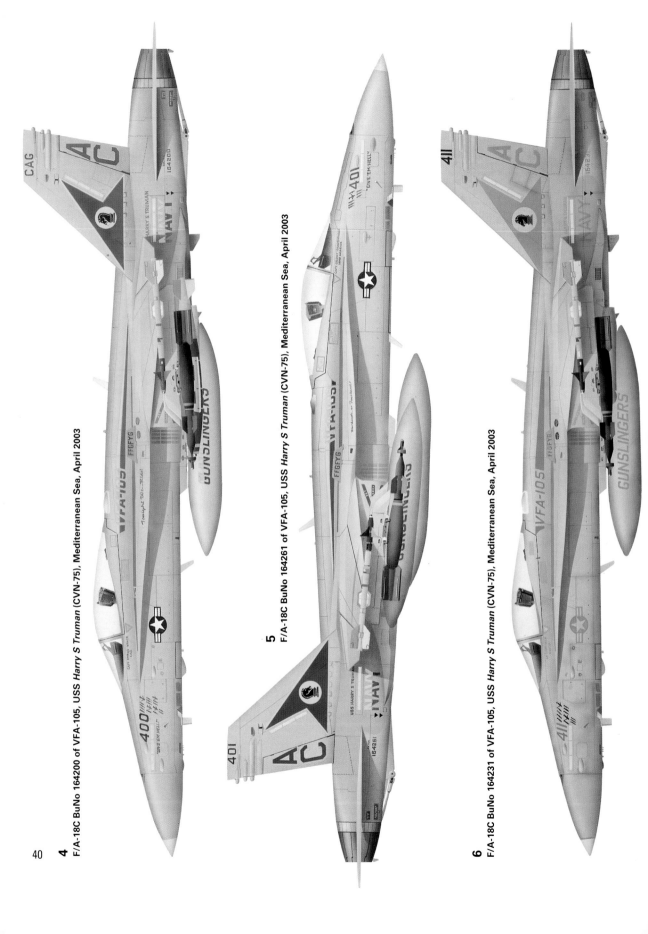

4

F/A-18C BuNo 164200 of VFA-105, USS *Harry S Truman* (CVN-75), Mediterranean Sea, April 2003

5

F/A-18C BuNo 164261 of VFA-105, USS *Harry S Truman* (CVN-75), Mediterranean Sea, April 2003

6

F/A-18C BuNo 164231 of VFA-105, USS *Harry S Truman* (CVN-75), Mediterranean Sea, April 2003

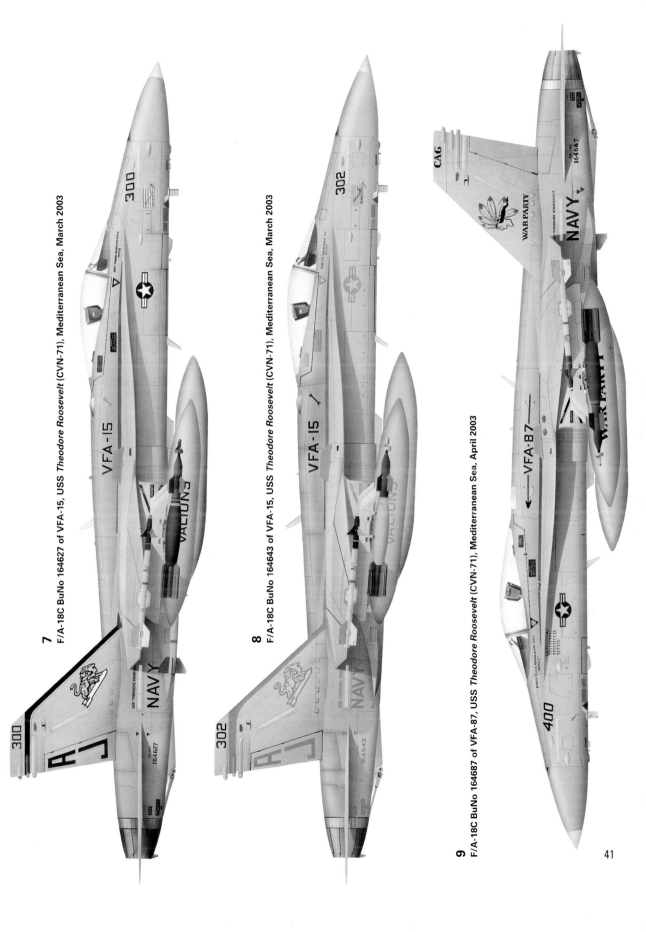

7

F/A-18C BuNo 164627 of VFA-15, USS *Theodore Roosevelt* (CVN-71), Mediterranean Sea, March 2003

8

F/A-18C BuNo 164643 of VFA-15, USS *Theodore Roosevelt* (CVN-71), Mediterranean Sea, March 2003

9

F/A-18C BuNo 164687 of VFA-87, USS *Theodore Roosevelt* (CVN-71), Mediterranean Sea, April 2003

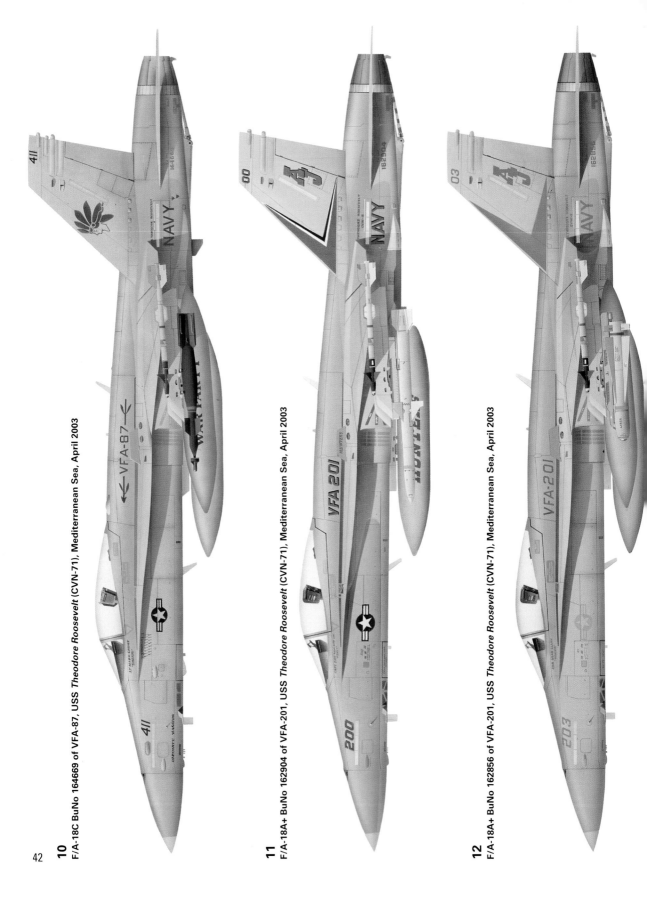

10
F/A-18C BuNo 164669 of VFA-87, USS *Theodore Roosevelt* (CVN-71), Mediterranean Sea, April 2003

11
F/A-18A+ BuNo 162904 of VFA-201, USS *Theodore Roosevelt* (CVN-71), Mediterranean Sea, April 2003

12
F/A-18A+ BuNo 162856 of VFA-201, USS *Theodore Roosevelt* (CVN-71), Mediterranean Sea, April 2003

4

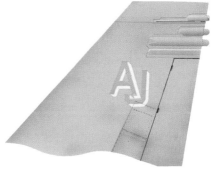

10

5

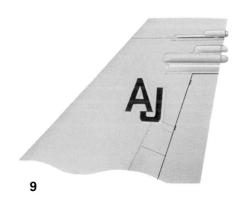

9

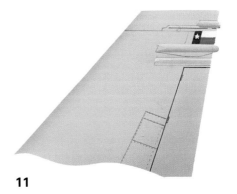

11

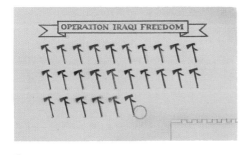

9

11

SOF CAS

As briefly mentioned earlier in this volume, the vast majority of the sorties conducted by CVW-3 and CVW-8 in OIF saw TACAIR assets flying in direct support of SOF and Kurdish Peshmerga militia forces on the ground. With three corps of Iraqi Army troops scattered throughout the region, the mission for the Coalition forces on the ground, supported by CTF-60's 72 Hornets and 20 Tomcats, was simple – keep the Iraqi troops occupied so that they could not head south to help defend Baghdad from the US Army's V Corps and the 1st Marine Expeditionary Force (MEF). The SOF squads operated throughout northern Iraq, and they were responsible for finding targets for the F/A-18s and F-14s.

Both air wings had spent the majority of their pre-cruise work-ups preparing for a conventional war that would see them flying tactical strikes and CAS missions for a large body of mechanised troops surging across the Turkish border into Iraq. This was exactly how the war was fought in the south (see *Combat Aircraft 46 – US Navy Hornet Units of Operation Iraqi Freedom Part One* for details), but with the 4th ID ruled out of the fight by the Turkish government, the CAOC was forced to change its plans for CTF-60. VFA-87's Cdr Greg Fenton, who spent five weeks working on the Navy's daily ATO in the CAOC at 'PSAB' in February-March 2003, summarised these changes for the author;

'For us fighting the war in the north, there were not a lot of pre-planned strikes when OIF commenced. What few we had were soon carried out, and then we switched our primary mission to supporting the ground forces that were arrayed along the "green line" – the boundary between the Kurdish area of northern Iraq and Iraqi-held territory. We had roughly 1000 SOF and 10,000 Kurdish Peshmerga militia fighters on the ground opposing somewhere between 100,000 and 120,000 Iraqi troops. Our job was to support the ground forces in the north, and that did not involve a lot of pre-planned strikes. Instead, we primarily flew CAS missions from 24 March until the campaign ended on 20 April.'

Right below
Harking back to Vietnam or *Desert Storm*, VFA-37's 'Bull 300' is armed with a single unguided Mk 83 general purpose (GP) bomb (fitted with a metallic blue M904E4 fuse in the nose) under each wing. Despite relying heavily on precision-guided ordnance, CVW-3's trio of Hornet units also dropped 37 500-lb Mk 82 and 86 1000-lb Mk 83 GP bombs. These could only be delivered in good weather, however, when pilots knew that they would be able to visually acquire the target prior to dropping their weapons. By comparison, the only unguided ordnance expended by CVW-8 in OIF were the 1218 20 mm cannon rounds fired by VFA-87 and VFA-201 (*Erik Lenten*)

Below
The KC-10As of the Bourgas-based 409th AEG were kept very busy by CTF-60 during OIF. The only Coalition aircraft based in Bulgaria, the Extenders were a vital asset in the northern campaign. The very last KC-10 delivered to the USAF, this particular jet (87-0124) is one of 32 Extenders assigned to the 305th Air Mobility Wing, based at McGuire AFB, New Jersey. It wears the blue fin stripe of the 2nd Air Refueling Squadron. The tanker's customer on this occasion is VFA-105's 'Canyon 411', which is still carrying its LGBs (*Cdr Tom Lalor*)

The transition from fixed target strikes to CAS happened quickly, and both CVW-3 and CVW-8 had to play 'catch up' a little in the first few days of the campaign in Op Area One. VFA-105's Lt Cdr Bradford Blackwelder recalled;

'The war started really slowly for my squadron in terms of ordnance coming off of our aircraft. When the planned invasion of the north by the 4th ID was blocked by the Turks, this meant that the carriers in the Mediterranean were going to have to carry more of the fight to the Iraqis than had originally been envisaged. This caught CVW-3 a little wrong footed, as we did not have enough guys up on deck ready to support the increased air asset requirement and rapid jet turnaround that was now being demanded. However, both the air wing and VFA-105 rose to the challenge, and by the end of OIF my unit had out-dropped everybody in CVW-3.'

The SOF squads were also caught cold by the late tactical change imposed on the Coalition in the north. Codenamed Task Force *Viking*, the Special Forces A teams of JSOTF-N had expected to fight their war in the same way as their compatriots in the south and west of Iraq, causing mayhem behind enemy lines by either destroying targets themselves, or designating them for destruction by TACAIR. This is, of course, how the *Viking* operatives conducted their business in the north, but without the luxury of 100,000+ Coalition troops advancing along a broad front, absorbing the pressure being exerted on SOF squads by the Iraqi Army.

V Corps and the 1st MEF also had plenty of work for the CTF-50 fighter-bombers, leaving SOF teams to pick out only the most high-value, or time-sensitive, targets for naval TACAIR. This was not the case in the north, as Lt Mike Kraus of VFA-105 explained;

'The switch from supporting a handful of invading mechanised infantry divisions, each of which controlled 15,000 troops, to operating exclusively with 1000 SOF guys overwhelmed the latter to some degree.

Above
Amongst CVW-3's first targets in OIF once CVN-75 had moved to Op Area One was Qayyarah West air base, south of Mosul. This photo shows exactly why naval aviators raved about JDAM – note the neat line of blackened craters in the two runways and the adjoining taxiways. One of 13 airfields either built from scratch or modernised by British and Yugoslavian contractors as part of Project *Super-Base* (which ran from 1975 through to 1987), Qayyarah West was created in the late 1970s. It was an immensely important airfield during the war with Iran in the 1980s, being the main hub for IrAF Mirage F1EQ operations, and also the first base to receive MiG-23MLs. MiG-25s were also operated from Qayyarah West later in the war. Finally, the IrAF's Northern Command secondary Sector Operations Center was based here until March 2003 (*VMFA-115*)

There were so few of them, and so many of us looking for targets. There were only so many secure radio frequencies, and we had 30 or 40 jets all trying to talk to the same people in order to get a tasking. It took four or five days to iron out the FAC wrinkles with these guys, but after that the CAS missions worked a lot better.'

A typical FAC team in the north consisted of just two SOF soldiers armed with a 0.50-cal sniper rifle and an all important Viper laser designator pod, the latter fitted with a x50 magnification scope. Both men would be wearing a mix of civilian and military attire, and they would usually team up with a Kurdish Peshmerga militiaman who was familiar with the local area in which they were operating.

Although these troops are actually airmen assigned to USAFE's RAF Mildenhall-based 100th Security Forces Squadron, which was airlifted in to protect Bashur airfield once it was seized by the 173rd Airborne Brigade, they are dressed and equipped in a similar fashion to the SOF FACs that provided TACAIR with its 'eyes on the ground' in OIF (*TSgt Rich Pucket*)

Working with FACs from different forces, and countries – British and Australian Special Air Service (SAS) FACs also saw action in northern Iraq – provided its own unique challenges for the TACAIR pilots in OIF. Navy and Marine FACs had been trained in NATO CAS techniques, but their US Army brethren had not been through the formalised CAS schools, nor had naval aviators trained with them pre-OIF. They were used to working with helicopters, which moved slower at lower altitudes when nearing targets. CVW-3 DCAG Capt Rainey recalled;

'The Army FACs were not well prepared for working with fast jets, and in the early stages of the conflict their controlling consisted of little more than calls such as "Here I am. Go and drop your bomb over there"! They often failed to give us any detailed coordinate specifics, which meant that we would then have to back them up and lead them through the prerequisite target specifics as per standard NATO CAS. You had to "push the pole" a little more in order to get the information you required.'

Lt Cdr Blackwelder experienced similar problems with an Army FAC on one of his early missions in the north;

'We had a guy tell us that the target was "on the hill" – a favourite call amongst ground controllers. After 15 fruitless minutes of searching for "the hill", I asked the FAC "How high is the hill?" He replied, "About 40 ft"! We were cruising at around 20,000 ft at the time. Some guys were simply more proficient than others, with most of the Army FACs – who we predominantly worked with – being more comfortable operating with slower rotary-winged platforms, rather than F/A-18s.'

BAD WEATHER

A further strain was placed on the FAC/TACAIR relationship in the north by the persistently bad weather that blighted many of the target areas in the early stages of the campaign. Conditions were at their worst on 24/25 March, although CTF-60 managed to generate a handful of sorties on both days. VFA-105's Cdr Lalor was an unexpected participant in the first SOF CAS mission flown from CVN-75 on the 24th;

Right
Topping off his tanks following his recent departure from CVN-75, the pilot of 'Canyon 410' holds his jet steady in the basket behind VS-22's 'Vidar 702' as both aircraft cruise over solid cloud. The first job for most CTF-60 Hornet pilots straight after launching would be to locate the duty Viking in the overhead above the carrier and take on 2000 lbs of fuel to replace what had been used during take-off. The longer-legged F-14s rarely made use of the S-3Bs, except perhaps to get back-side gas if the marshall pattern was busy upon their return home at the end of a lengthy FAC(A) mission (*Cdr Tom Lalor*)

'On that first day in the north, I was scheduled to be the turning spare jet for a dozen-aircraft package led by CAG Vance. We were tasked to support a SOF team about ten miles northeast of Kirkuk. As we each started our aircraft in the pre-dawn darkness of the crowded flight deck, I looked over at CAG's Tomcat and saw a number of maintenance technicians working feverishly to repair a hydraulic problem. Within a few minutes CAG came over the radio and reported that his aircraft was down, and that I was to launch in his place as the alternate strike lead.

'Once airborne, I struggled to find my two wingmen in the thick cloud cover that almost entirely obscured the airspace above the carrier. After much difficulty picking our way through the weather, we all joined on the S-3B tanker and onloaded another 2000 lbs of fuel, before starting on our way across southern Turkey. Flying northeast over the Mediterranean,

Above
The pilot of 'Canyon 407' prepares to leave the rain-soaked flightdeck of 'HST' behind him as he engages afterburner seconds prior to launching from bow cat one on 24 March 2003. Lot XIII F/A-18C BuNo 164253 is carrying a single 1000-lb GBU-32(V)2 JDAM beneath its port wing. Note also that the jet has had its near-mandatory NITE Hawk pod removed in favour of an AIM-120C AMRAAM – this 'bad weather' configuration was only seen during the 'Shock and Awe' phase of OIF (*PHAN Carl E Gibson*)

we coasted in over Turkey near the city of Adana. The weather continued to worsen as we headed east, and soon we found ourselves with our engines at nearly full power struggling to lift our heavy bomb loads above the cloud cover at almost 40,000 ft!

'It was a fantastic sight, skimming above the misty cloud tops, with a deep indigo sky above us and three perfectly parallel brilliant white contrails magically forming behind our Hornets. But for all its splendour, it meant accepting some serious risks.

'Firstly, in the very thin atmosphere at this altitude, our engines had only enough power to keep the aircraft just above stalling speed. As soon as we attempted to turn sharply our jets would buffet, signalling an impending stall. We were in and out of afterburner just to hold altitude. It was like walking on ice – if you tried to make a sudden move, you were likely to end up flipped over on your back. Secondly, with the clouds just a few hundred feet below us, we would have no reaction time to try to avoid any incoming SAMs that might be shot at us. Thirdly, we would be bombing completely blind.

'One critical aspect of CAS is the ability of the FAC to talk the pilot's eyes onto the target. With the cloud cover solid from 5000 ft up to almost 35,000 ft, we would have to programme his coordinates into our 1000-lb JDAM and release on pure faith. It was the ultimate in trust – the FAC on the ground trusted us to get our coordinates entered in correctly, and we trusted that the coordinates he gave us were accurate. The consequences of getting it wrong could be catastrophic – either hitting innocent civilians or our own forces.

'Less than a year earlier, a SOF soldier in Afghanistan had accidentally passed his own position rather than that of the target to the pilot. Unfortunately the bomb worked as designed, with lethal precision. Even though it was not the pilot's fault, none of us could imagine the guilt he must have felt knowing that he had accidentally taken the life of a fellow Coalition soldier.

'But the last challenge presented by the weather was the most nerve racking – that of finding the Air Force tankers holding at about 20,000 ft in solid cloud cover. The three KC-135 refuellers were stacked at 2000-ft intervals, orbiting over northern Iraq. Like us, they too were unable to find any clear air in which to work. As we let down into the murky grey abyss, I scanned my air-to-air radar, looking for any other "customers" that might be in the same piece of sky trying to do the same thing that we were. Typically, a tanker will already have two to four receivers on the wing, waiting for their turn to refuel.

'As we carefully closed the distance on the small radar return displayed on the screen, I subconsciously hunched myself down in the cockpit, trying to get a little

VFA-105 CO Cdr Tom Lalor was CVW-3's senior squadron commander during OIF, and he led the air wing's second 'Shock and Awe' strike. He is seen here with 'Canyon 401' (armed with a personalised GBU-12) on 10 April 2003, just prior to flying one of his 19 combat missions (*Cdr Tom Lalor*)

smaller, as if that would help ward off the impending collision! I watched the range creep down. The huge airliner converted into a tanker was out there in front of us somewhere. The gap closed – 2 miles, 1.5, 1.0, still nothing . . . Finally, at about half-a-mile, a large dark grey silhouette slowly appeared out of the gloom. As it eventually formed the shape of the familiar KC-135, I noticed a pair of Hornets already sitting in position off the big aeroplane's left wing. Only by pure luck did we not collide somewhere over the snow-covered mountains of Iraq as we both blindly rendezvoused on the same aircraft.

'It was a great relief when the last member of my flight had finished refuelling and we climbed back up into the brilliant sunlight, ready to get on with our business.

'The space between about 37,000 ft and 40,000 ft was jam-packed with Coalition aircraft in holding patterns as they waited to be paired with their ground controllers. I remember at one point a B-52 joined the crowd, the leviathan gracefully soaring above us loaded with dozens of bombs on the pylons under its wings. The bomber passed barely 1000 ft over us, dwarfing our little fighters. As I marvelled at the scene, I remember thinking that no enemy would stand a chance against that much firepower. It was an amazing sight.

'We did not have much time to enjoy the view, however. A CVW-3 E-2C directed us to contact a FAC, whose call-sign was "Incur Tango", on one of the encrypted CAS frequencies. After several calls, the radio finally crackled back with a response. It was an American voice on the other end of the line. Whether he was Army SOF or CIA, or some other "snake eater", I will never know. He sounded like he had been around the block once or twice, and was used to penetrating deep into enemy territory with minimal equipment, cut off for miles from the nearest friendly forces. Still, in spite of his cool professionalism, we could tell from his breathlessness and the tone of his voice that he was in close contact with Iraqi forces. "Incur Tango" was exchanging fire with Iraqi Republican Guard soldiers occupying a building on the outskirts of a nearby village.

'Our FAC explained that the enemy was massing for an attack against his position, and he was in danger of being overrun. He quickly passed us the precision coordinates of the building and we read them back. I then asked him for his desired time on target, and his response spoke volumes. "How quickly can you get here?" "We're inbound now" was my reply.

'My wingmen and I furiously typed in the coordinates for our bombs as we approached our release point. We read back the position to each other so as to verify that each of us had not made a mistake and entered in the wrong numbers. We finished our cross-checks just prior to reaching the release point and got our JDAM off as expeditiously as we could.

'I noted the time of fall computed in the Hornet's weapons computer – 62 seconds. That minute felt more like an hour as we waited to hear from our partner on the ground. The minute passed, but we got no response. I keyed the mike: "'Incur Tango', this is 'Mako 05', how do you hear?" Silence. "'Incur Tango', this is 'Mako 05', radio check". Nothing but static on the other end. I started to feel sick to my stomach. We had had radio contact with him right up until the computed bomb impact time. Had something gone wrong? My mind raced with the possibilities.

Maybe we were too late and he was overrun by Iraqi troops. Or maybe one of us had typed in bad coordinates and put our bombs into his position.

'Within a few minutes I was working to suppress a low-grade panic. Was I going to be the cause of the first deaths by friendly fire? To make matters worse, we were beginning to get low on fuel and had to rejoin on the tanker. I once again had to descend into the cloud cover below, with my two squadronmates hanging onto my wingtips. Picking our way through the fog, we relied on little more than the law of averages to keep us from colliding with other aircraft joining at the same time. This time though our tanker had managed to find a thin layer of clear air, and we thankfully joined up as quickly as we could before losing him in the goo.

'I grabbed my gas and moved out to the right side of the KC-135 while I waited for my two wingmen to do the same. With my tanking complete, my mind immediately returned to "Incur Tango". The suspense was agonising. I had to know that he was all right. Holding my position on the big jet's wingtip, I switched back to the FAC's frequency and tried once more. "'Incur Tango', this is 'Mako 05', how do you hear?" This time, to my great relief, the reply was instant, and actually sounded cheery.

"'Mako' this is 'Incur Tango', go ahead!" Thank God! "Hey, where have you been?" I half-shouted over the radio. "We have been trying to reach you for the last 15 minutes! You gave us a hell of a scare!" He replied sheepishly "Uh, sorry about that. We had to reposition to take cover from your bombs and couldn't talk. They were direct hits – right on the building. Estimate 50-100 KIA". We hadn't screwed it up. What a relief!

'Although we never came under enemy fire ourselves on that sortie, between the weather and the apparent bombing mistake, it was easily the most terrifying of the 19 missions I completed in OIF.'

Lt Cdr Blackwelder was flying in Cdr Lalor's all-VFA-105 section during this mission;

'My first OIF sortie, flown with Skipper Lalor and Lt Mike Kraus, was a "goat rope" in all honesty because of the poor weather. Indeed, the first week-and-a-half of the war was dominated by a series of weather fronts that moved in off the Mediterranean and simply sat over Turkey and

The KC-135R/Ts of the 319th ARW, based at Grand Forks AFB, North Dakota, were also forward-deployed to the Akrotiri FLOS to serve with the 401st ARW for the duration of OIF. This aircraft (57-1440), from the 912th ARS, is refuelling an F/A-18C from VFA-105 at dawn over the Turkey-Iraq border on 8 April 2003. Standard operational procedure within the US armed forces states that the tanker's flying boom operator requires at least a mile's visibility before refuelling can safely take place. However, the one mile rule was occasionally ignored when thirsty Hornets went looking for gas in poor weather at night during OIF (Cdr Tom Lalor)

northern Iraq. As far as we knew, the cloud stretched solidly from the surface up to around 40,000 ft. Despite being completely socked in, CTF-60 had daily ATOs to carry out and FAC teams that were relying exclusively on our aerial support, which meant wave after wave of jets left the carrier and headed east to meet their USAF tankers over Turkey.

'Once over land, you found that all the tankers were stacked up in the clouds. So now you had all these tactical jets trying find *their* tanker. The KC-135s were flying a standard racetrack pattern between 20,000 and 25,000 ft, just a mile in trail of each other. With tactical jets usually heading for Iraq at around 40,000 ft so as to stay above the clouds, we had to descend into the murk in order to find our all-important tankers. There we were 600 miles from the carrier, in cloud and trying to find gas!

'Having at last refuelled, we climbed back up out of the clouds and got on with flying our CAS mission. We were all carrying JDAM, which was nice, and the SOF guy on the ground fed us coordinates for targets that he had picked out. Ironically, the bombing aspect of the mission proved to be the easiest part of the sortie in the early stages of OIF.'

Lt Mike Kraus also has vivid memories of these early sorties;

'We were flying around at 35,000 ft over the target area, and the AWACS controllers were frantically trying to separate everyone by altitude so that you could go and do your own thing with your FAC without the fear of having a mid-air collision with another jet from CVW-3. When conducting such missions at Fallon, for example, we would have a 15,000-ft window that would see formations working between 25,000 ft and 40,000 ft. However, with the weather not clearing until you got above 32,000 ft, everybody was working in a 5000-ft window between 35,000 ft and 40,000 ft!

'This meant that we were having to dodge other Hornets and Tomcats, work on dropping bombs on targets that you couldn't see on the instruction of a FAC, and also talk on the radio to pilots nearby who were also out of sight so as to avoid running into them.

Its hull rust-streaked after weeks of uninterrupted 'blue water ops', *Theodore Roosevelt* sails through a rain squall in Op Area One at the end of another night's OIF flying. All of CVW-8's aircraft are safely back down on deck, despite the weather, and the hard-pressed maintenance crews have already started work rectifying and readying airframes for the following night. Once the plane guard H-60 Seahawk lands, 'TR's' air boss will declare the flightdeck closed and OIF mission responsibility will pass to CTF-60's day carrier, CVN-75 (*PHAN Todd M Flint*)

'My first mission on 24 March lasted four hours and forty-five minutes, of which around three-and-half-hours were spent on instruments. For much of this sortie my eyes darted between the instruments and the reflective slime strips on my leader's jet. The concentration levels were at their highest when we were trying to find gas, or a clear break in the clouds in order to fight off attacks of vertigo, when you thought that the jet was upside down. You can also get shot down a lot more easily by an unguided SAM in cloud, as you clearly cannot see its telltale plume.

'There was lot of frustration in the cockpits of our jets early on due to the poor weather, and the effect it was having on our ability to fly the missions tasked. We were very happy when the weather cleared.'

CVW-8 also had to contest with the poor weather, but to make matters worse irs crews were flying at night. Although conditions had been bad for CVW-3 during the hours of daylight on 24 March, that evening the cloud cover became so thick that the strike lead of the first package launched by CVW-8 from Op Area One called the mission off mid-flight. VFA-15's Cdr Lewis remembered;

'This strike was led by my good mate, and CO of VFA-87, Cdr Dave Morgan. He took his package to the tankers in really bad weather and made the mature decision to turn everyone around. Although he was disappointed to not be able to execute the mission that night, his decision set the tone for our operations. Mission success was critical, but it was not worth losing an aeroplane or killing a friendly on the ground because we wanted to "get in the game". My "nuggets", like their counterparts throughout the air wing, also impressed me time and again by making mature decisions in the heat of the moment. They were tactically sound, but more importantly, they avoided making dumb mistakes.'

CVW-8 CAG Capt Newland was also worried about how his junior pilots would fare in the poor weather that blighted Turkey and northern Iraq on 24-25 March;

'As CAG, some of my toughest decisions in OIF centred on sending those first few strikes into northern Iraq after we had moved to Op Area One. The weather really was awful, and on those first couple of nights I had "JOs" hanging onto the wings of their flight leads. Nobody had ever seen tanking in the clouds at 35,000 ft. It is just not good to be going to a place where they are shooting at you, and you are in full cloud flying on instruments and NVGs. The bottom line in my decision-making on these early missions was that we were supporting the guys on the ground, so we went ahead and flew the sorties regardless of the weather.

'I still can't quite work out how those junior Hornet pilots managed to fly at night, in bad weather, on NVGs, on the wing of somebody else, and still work the radios, let alone put bombs accurately on a target. Indeed, the LGB aspect of the mission is pretty intensive too. Yet they did, night after night. Thank God the Hornet is a great aeroplane to fly, because if it was not, then they really would have had their hands full!'

The weather had not improved over Turkey or northern Iraq by dawn on 25 March, forcing CTF-60 commander, Rear Adm John Stufflebeem (who was embarked with his staff in CVN-75), to shut down *Harry S Truman*'s deck for a full 24 hours when he deemed conditions to be too bad for safe flight. The Rear Admiral explained his decision to the embedded press aboard the vessel;

'We launched two missions this morning (25th), and they were unable to reach their target so they returned back to the ship safely. The weather is bad enough that we can't get to the (refuelling) tankers, and because of the lousy weather, we are not getting the coordination on the ground that we need to have to release the weapons.'

Despite CVW-3 failing to get any jets over Iraq on 25 March, that evening conditions had improved sufficiently enough for CVW-8 to launch a single wave of Hornets and Tomcats, supported by Prowlers, against several FAC-identified targets. A total of 18 JDAM (four 2000-lb GBU-31(V)2s, carried by two F-14D from VF-213, and 14 1000-lb GBU-35(V)1s, dropped by six F/A-18s) were expended.

The morning of the 26th was ushered in with winds that cleared out much of the inclement weather. The day dawned with vivid blue skies, and despite the breezy conditions, Stufflebeem stated that refuelling operations were not being hindered by turbulence. 'The visibility is very good, and the aircraft can come down in altitude, and the tankers can in turn find those altitudes where turbulence is minimised', the Rear Admiral told the press corps in his daily conference aboard CVN-75.

AIRDROP SUPPORT

It was just as well that the weather cleared when it did, for in a perfect example of inter-service operability, during the night of 26/27 March CVW-8 provided DCA and CAS support for the airborne assault on Bashur air base, near Irbil, by 1000 paratroopers of the US Army's 173rd Airborne Brigade. Conducting the largest parachute drop since the invasion of Panama (Operation *Just Cause*) in December 1989, the soldiers jumped from 15 USAF C-17 Globemaster IIs that were escorted by three waves of strike aircraft from CVW-8.

The Air Mobility Command C-17s from the 62nd and 437th Airlift Wings had loaded up and launched from Aviano air base, in Italy, each transport refuelling twice en route to Iraq. Despite the poor weather, the Globemaster IIs succeeded in rendezvousing with their Tomcat, Hornet and Prowler escorts shortly after tanking for the last time. Cdr Sean Clark of VFA-201 was one of the strike leads for CVW-8;

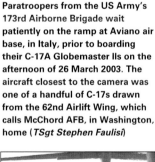

Paratroopers from the US Army's 173rd Airborne Brigade wait patiently on the ramp at Aviano air base, in Italy, prior to boarding their C-17A Globemaster IIs on the afternoon of 26 March 2003. The aircraft closest to the camera was one of a handful of C-17s drawn from the 62nd Airlift Wing, which calls McChord AFB, in Washington, home (*TSgt Stephen Faulisi*)

'The guys on the ground were always our top priority in OIF, and never more so than during the initial para-insertion of the 173rd in the north. When giving my pre-mission brief on the 26th, I made it perfectly clear to my package that we would fly and fight regardless of the poor weather conditions expected over the target. This was emphatically supported by Rear Adm John Harvey, Commander, *Theodore Roosevelt* Strike Group, who sat in on my brief and told each and every one of us at the conclusion of my presentation that "our troops on the ground could literally die if we didn't support them! This is no longer a training mission. This is combat, gentlemen!" Rear Adm Harvey then pulled me aside and told me that my strike was to "give the Iraqis hell" and help the SOF guys in harm's way on the ground.'

VFA-15's Executive Officer, Cdr Ed Langford, was an element lead for the first wave of jets sortied by CVW-8 in support of the drop;

'That mission was a real eye opener, and it was again a high-risk

operation that was thoroughly briefed beforehand. The 173rd carried out a pretty sporty jump, as the Air Force had to get 1000 guys onto an airfield situated in a fairly mountainous part of northern Iraq. To make matters worse, the weather was not very good – I for one would not have wanted to jump out of an aeroplane into it! On the NVGs, we could see a string of 15 C-17s disgorging their human cargo. Again, we were given permission by the CAOC to do whatever it took to make sure that these guys got onto the ground safely and took control of the airfield.'

Flying as Cdr Langford's wingman on this mission was one of VFA-15's seven 'nugget' pilots, Lt(jg) Jon Biehl;

'My very first OIF sortie was the escort mission for the C-17 drop on Bashur airfield, Cdr Langford and I each flying a Hornet armed with three GBU-35(V)1 JDAM apiece. Although the weather that night was expected to be bad, the drop went ahead as planned. We were assigned a kill box to work over in order to fly CAS for the insertion, and had no pre-planned targets. I still remember the adrenalin that was pumping around my body as I walked out to my jet, strapped in and launched. Although this was my first combat mission I wasn't scared, just excited.

'The flight over Turkey en route to Iraq seemed to go quickly, and before I knew it I was watching my XO refuel in the clouds at night. There was a lot of turbulence. He eventually got his probe into the tanker's

Despite concerns that the weather might not allow the air drop to take place, the 173rd's 1000 paratroopers boarded their C-17s and departed Aviano on schedule. This 'sky soldier' is laden down with his parachute pack and combat survival equipment. Note the padding on his knees and elbows (*A1C Isaac G L Freeman*)

CDR ED LANGFORD XO
CLYDE

While the paratroopers were boarding their transports for a one-way trip to Bashur air base, the naval aviators charged with ensuring their safe arrival over the drop zone were also manning up their aircraft aboard CVN-71. One of those involved in the mission was VFA-15 'nugget' pilot Lt(jg) Jon Biehl. Flying as wingman to squadron XO Cdr Ed Langford, Biehl – who was conducting his first OIF sortie – was assigned his section leader's named jet ('Valion 302') for the mission (*Lt(jg) Jon Biehl*)

The pilot of 'Valion 306' (Lot XIV F/A-18C BuNo 164691) has engaged afterburner and switched on his position lights and 'slime strips' in preparation for a night launch from 'TR's' waist cat three on 27 March 2003. The jet carries a single GBU-12 beneath its starboard wing (*PHAN Brad Garner*)

trailing basket, but I began to worry because it was my turn next. He topped off and pulled out. I then began a refuelling evolution that I'll never forget.

'As I stabilised behind the KC-135, the basket was flopping around like a fish on a hook. An eternity seemed to go by as I kept stabbing my probe at the "Iron Maiden" (the nickname given to the KC-135's heavy basket, which has a habit of ripping probes off and damaging the Navy jets' refuelling probe doors – author) in the hope that it would catch it. At least five minutes had now passed, and I had still not plugged in. It had never taken me this long to get into the basket at any previous stage in my brief Hornet career, and with the basket seeming unlikely to settle down anytime soon, I began to wonder if I was ever going to get gas!

'It was at this point that I realised that I had to do whatever was necessary to get into that damn basket. I calmed myself down and eventually got in. As I saw the numbers on my fuel gauge begin to rise, I noticed that I had started to breathe again. Then I remembered that I had to refuel two more times that night!

'Once I was done, my flight lead flew us to our kill box near Bashur airfield, where we were given our FAC's frequency – open channel radio instructions never consisted of the frequency by its actual numbers due to security concerns. Instead, we were given code names like "BLUE 16" or "BEIGE 24". These could be deciphered by referring to our kneeboard pack, which we hastily rummaged through in order to find them.

'We eventually contacted our FAC and told him that we were a flight of two Hornets with three JDAM each. He immediately began giving us instructions and coordinates for our first target. My skipper and I were given different coordinates for two targets that were in the same vicinity. Having copied down the numbers, I looked out of my cockpit through my NVGs and saw the unforgettable sight of 15 C-17s transporting the 173rd Airborne Brigade in the direction of Bashur.

'While I hung on to my lead's wing as we flew through scattered clouds, I typed the precise coordinates for my target – a revetment filled with Iraqi troops – into the jet's bomb computer. We flew to the drop point and released our JDAM uneventfully. A short while later we headed back to our tanker track for mid-cycle refuelling, and this proved to be much easier the second time round.

'All of my subsequent OIF missions – I flew nine in total – had the same flow to them. Our ordnance load out may have varied, but the means by which we employed our weapons remained the same.'

The Hornet and Tomcat pilots who witnessed the airdrop found it a truly sobering experience. They were only too aware that these troops, devoid of any real mechanised support on the ground and operating deep inside enemy territory, would be relying almost exclusively on TACAIR in the coming days to keep the Iraqi Army at bay as they pushed out to attack targets around Tikrit, Kirkuk and Mosul.

All of the CVW-8 aircraft that had launched as escorts for the C-17s were armed with a mixed load-out of air-to-air missiles, JDAM and, for the first time in OIF, LGBs. The crews were more than ready to support the landings should they be resisted either from the air or the ground, but there were no enemy forces to be seen. As VFA-15's Lt Biehl recounted, the Hornet and Tomcat crews eventually left the area and dropped their bombs on some kill box targets around Kirkuk once the transports had headed back into Turkey.

Three waves of strike aircraft from CVN-75 that launched at dawn in support of the 173rd's landings also struck kill box targets in the form of command and control bunkers and troop and artillery positions close to Bashur airfield when they too found no 'trade' near Irbil.

Although the campaign in the north was dominated by FAC-controlled CAS, the missions flown by CVW-3 and CVW-8 in the immediate aftermath of the Bashur airfield assault were proof positive that both air wings continued to strike fixed targets that did not require direct talk-on by a SOF operative on the ground. DCAG Capt Rainey explained why such attacks were flown right up until war's end;

'Due to movement of FACs on the ground, poor weather or a lack of pre-planned targets, on occasion there were not enough targets to go around. You would know about this pretty quickly upon checking in with your AWACS controller, so you would remain at altitude and wait for

Lt(jg) Jon Biehl took this photograph from the cockpit of 'Valion 302' while waiting to launch on one of the nine missions that he completed during OIF. Biehl's element lead, Cdr Ed Langford, can be seen being marshalled towards the stern of CVN-71 in 'Valion 314' as he prepares to take his place in the queue behind the waist cats. Lot XIV F/A-18C BuNo 164657 is armed with a single GBU-35(V)1 and GBU-12 beneath its port wing, the jet almost certainly carrying a solitary JDAM or LGB on its outer starboard wing pylon too (Lt(jg) Jon Biehl)

some tasking. Typically, we would then ask for kill boxes to be opened south of the "green line" as part of our secondary Kill box Interdiction/Close Air Support (KI/CAS) tasking. If you did not have a pre-planned target, and you could open up and start working a kill box, you could still find plenty of targets to drop your ordnance on without having to rely on a ground FAC.

'Pre-war, we had our CAG AI (Intel) survey all the planned kill boxes – between 40 and 50 – in northern Iraq for hardened sites so we knew where all the bunkers and revetments were inside these areas prior to the conflict commencing. From north of Mosul all the way south to K2 airfield, we knew where the targets were, and if we could get those kill boxes open without any possibility of fratricide or collateral damage, we would go ahead and prosecute them in preference to hauling our bombs back to the ship.

'One example of a fixed target that CVW-3 hit regularly was a huge bunker complex within a kill box north of Mosul which was on the right side of the "green line". We were able to work in there without any restriction. South of Kirkuk, Iraqi corps division armour was scattered throughout the region, and if you went far enough south of town it was all Republican Guard and headquarters barracks. More often than not, you would also have Intel imagery and coordinates on reveted HQ buildings in the area too.

'If we were working near Kirkuk, and there was no FAC tasking, we would ask our controller to open up "95 Alpha" in "Keypad Seven", which was a specific area of that kill box. He would in turn call the CAOC, who would call the SOF guys, and the latter would coordinate with their teams in the field to find out if they had any friendlies in the area. Within ten to 15 minutes we would get a reply telling us that it was either opened or closed – if the latter, then you knew they had SOF teams working in the area.

'After a week of operating in this way, you became pretty adept at knowing where the targets were, where you could and couldn't work and what had and had not been hit.

'Kill box familiarity was high in CVW-3, as we usually sortied with the same group of guys every time. I typically flew with Team Two on the first event of the morning. That meant I would get up at 0300 hrs, launch by 0500 hrs and be back by 1300 hrs. I would then eat and brief/debrief upon my return. CAG Vance and I would do a situational exchange via e-mail, and he would leave notes on his desk and then go fly while I "watched the fort". One of us had to be on board the ship at all times. However, there was usually enough gouge (information) amongst the squadrons in the ready rooms to get most missions done without our direct input on whether it was workable or not.'

Getting permission to bomb targets independently of direct FAC control could be a less than straightforward task for naval aviators in the north, as Coalition commanders were mortified at the thought of 'blue-on-blue' fratricide occurring on the same scale as it had done in *Desert Storm*. VFA-87's Cdr Fenton detailed the processes that had to be followed before a pilot could begin working over a kill box;

'At times we would launch with alternate targets programmed into our bomb computers should none of the FACs need air support once we got

over northern Iraq. We still needed permission to bomb these alternate targets, however, and this only came after we had orbited several times on station over the primary target area without getting a tasking from a FAC. Once we had permission to strike the alternate targets, we would go and bomb them using our own self-lasing capabilities.

'Communicating up north was tough, and to get permission to operate independently of a FAC you had to get on the radio and talk to an E-2, or an E-3 if there was one operating in the area. They in turn would communicate with the CAOC at "PSAB" via satellite link and obtain permission for you to strike the particular target you had identified. This approval would then be radioed back to us by the AWACS controller. We usually got a turnaround on such a target request within 10-15 minutes.'

KI/CAS

The KI/CAS tactic that was used to great effect in the more conventional campaign fought in the south, but which also played an important part in the northern offensive, had been devised by CAOC planners pre-war. Senior strategists had realised in the months leading up to OIF that TACAIR assets would run out of fixed targets in Iraq within a matter of days should 'Shock and Awe' go to plan. CENTCOM staffers soon decided that the best way to make use of aircraft equipped with JDAM and LGBs, but without a specific mission to fly (either FAC-controlled

'Party 411' (Lot XIV F/A-18C BuNo 164669) comes under tension on 'TR's' waist cat three on 13 April 2003. The jet boasts a typical northern front configuration of two external tanks and bombs on three pylons. VFA-87's Cdr Greg Fenton explained why this fit was used;

'We adopted the "hard wing" configuration, with a tank under the wing and on the centreline, because it allowed us to carry a greater range of weaponry and still be able to bring this ordnance back in the event that it was not expended. Such a load out has no effect on the jet's handling when the fuel tanks are empty, but when they are full the pilot has to deal with a number of asymmetric load issues. We would have preferred to have loaded a tank under each wing and ordnance on the centreline and outer wing pylons, but in wartime we always have to go with the "hard wing" configuration' (*PHAN Aaron Burden*)

Lot XIV F/A-18C BuNo 164643 'Valion 302', with Cdr Langford at the controls, circles a recently bombed target in northern Iraq during the final days of OIF. CVW-8 conducted a limited number of daylight missions towards the end of the campaign, jets launching just prior to sunrise and entering Iraqi airspace soon after dawn. In these VFR conditions, with excellent visibility from 30,000 ft, the 500-lb GBU-12D/B LGB was the weapon of choice (*Lt(jg) Jon Biehl*)

CAS or against a pre-briefed, fixed target), was to switch their focus to KI/CAS and Battlefield Air Interdiction (BAI).

Considerable thought had gone into how best to control TACAIR assets in OIF once the invasion had commenced, with Gen Tommy Franks challenging his planners to integrate as many air assets as they could into an overall network of 'joint fires' that supported ground force commanders. The CAOC's mission planning team duly came up with the Fire Control Support Line (FCSL), which delineated a moving line up to which the 'joint fire' assets – jets, attack helicopters and artillery – were under the control of ground commanders in the field, and beyond which they fell under the jurisdiction of the Joint Force Air Component Commander (JFACC).

This was a radical plan, as traditionally all strike aircraft had been controlled solely by the JFACC in a time of conflict. Gen Franks placed even more faith in his senior officers on the ground by opting for a 'deep FCSL' once OIF commenced, this seeing Army or Marine divisional commanders controlling all 'joint fires' out to a range of 100 miles.

In an effort to allow the JFACC to play its part in the 'deep FCSL' strategy, CENTCOM devised the kill box system. This saw a ground commander split up his area of responsibility into 18.5-mile x 18.5-mile boxes, which he would then declare 'closed' when his troops entered them. Such a system shifted the 'joint fires' responsibility from the JFACC to the ground commander, thus reducing the chance of 'blue-on-blue' fratricide. When a box was declared 'open', the JFACC would assume that it was clear of friendly forces, thus allowing Coalition TACAIR to prosecute enemy targets.

The FSCL tactic was not applied in its truest sense in the north, as there was never a clear moving line up to which Coalition forces had progressed. By the very nature of the guerrilla war being fought by SOF and Kurdish Peshmerga fighters in this theatre, naval aviators could only be sure of the exact location of friendly troops when conducting CAS missions by being in radio contact with them as they attacked the targets that they had been instructed to. Within an hour the friendlies could have moved away from the area, which would revert to Iraqi control again.

Despite the hit-and-run nature of the northern war, and the overall lack of ground occupation by Coalition forces until the final days of the conflict, the SOF JFACC nevertheless enjoyed great success 'shaping his battlefield' in advance of mechanised troops attacking cities such as Mosul, Kirkuk and Tikrit in mid April. He achieved this by requesting CAOC-controlled BAI sorties against troop concentrations held in reserve, reveted armour around these conurbations and the selective destruction of bridges. The latter strikes in particular stopped the Iraqi Army's 15th Mechanised Division and other Republican Guard forces in the area from heading south to help bolster the defence of Baghdad.

Left
While CVW-8 waged war at night, CVW-3's maintainers worked through the hours of darkness readying aircraft for the following day's missions over northern Iraq. Here, aircraft handlers use a dedicated hangar tractor to move an F/A-18C from VFA-37 towards one of the deck elevators following the completion of rectification work aboard CVN-75 (*PH1 Michael W Pendergrass*)

One such BAI anti-bridge mission ordered directly by the CAOC was led by VFA-15's Cdr Ed Langford on 2 April, and involved jets from all three of CVW-8's Hornet units, as well as two F-14Ds from VF-213;

'In late March we received intelligence that Iraqi mechanised forces were starting to move south in an effort to reinforce Baghdad, and the CAOC identified that there were bridges in Tikrit that needed to be brought down in order to cut off the enemy's access south through this key city. CVW-8 was told that these bridges needed to be dropped as expeditiously as possible, but without inflicting collateral damage because of their location in a built-up area of the city. This was a high-risk mission for us both in terms of what would happen if our bombs missed the target, and the poor weather that blighted the area during this period – the defensive threat was also unknown.

'All the appropriate clearances were in place from high up to allow us to attack these bridges. I was the strike lead for this mission, and we duly hit the bridges with pinpoint accuracy. What we did not know was that there was a natural gas pipeline beneath one of them, and it split open and exploded when the bombs hit!

'By the time we finished taking down the last bridge we were *below* the AAA that was being fired at us in ever increasing volume, and our jets were glowing from the lights of the city. We had been forced to attack at a lower altitude than we would have preferred, having to get underneath the weather so as to accurately lase our GBU-10 2000-lb LGBs, which were the weapons of choice for these high-risk targets due to their proven span-dropping ability.

'Tikrit was very much in the heart of "bad guy" country at the time, which meant no FACs on the ground. We had to rely exclusively on self-contained lasing with the Hornet's NITE Hawk pod, or use the vastly superior AN/AAQ-25 LANTIRN Targeting System pods carried by the two F-14Ds from VF-213, which played a key part in this strike.'

This mission by CVW-8 was the only time that the GBU-10 was employed in anger by CTF-60 in OIF. Indeed, this specialist deep penetration bomb which had proven so popular in *Desert Storm* against bridges, Scud missiles, command, control, communications and intelligence nodes and bunkers was hardly used at all by the Navy in OIF, either in the north or the south.

BUDDY-LASING

Both self- and buddy-lasing really came into their own in northern Iraq, where TACAIR assets would often be attacking targets in kill boxes independently of any local laser-designator-equipped SOF FAC support. Every Tomcat and Hornet in OIF was equipped with a bolt-on laser designator pod which allowed the aircraft to successfully 'paint' their targets with guidance energy for their LGBs.

The workload for the pilot in a single-seat Hornet was typically at its highest during the lead up to a bombing attack with an LGB, and the additional responsibility of self-lasing a well-hidden, or moving, target in marginal weather stretched the naval aviator's manual dexterity to near breaking point. Therefore, whenever possible, the Hornet pilot would work out his attack profile and leave the laser target designation to either his wingman or a Tomcat operating with his section. The latter aircraft, being dual-crewed, also took on the increasingly important Forward Air Controller (Airborne) mission from where it had left off in OEF.

Navy and Marine Corps units have always been great proponents of working with FACs strapped into fast jet types. Known as Forward Air Controller (Airborne), the lineage of the FAC(A) goes back to Vietnam, when Marine 'spotters' performed Tactical Air Controlling (Airborne) tasks in aircraft such as the TF-9J Cougar and TA-4F Skyhawk. Today, the Marines conduct the FAC(A) mission from their two-seat F/A-18Ds, which proved indispensable in the ground campaign of OIF (see *Osprey Combat Aircraft 56 – US Marine and RAAF Hornet Units of Operation Iraqi Freedom* for further details).

The Navy embraced FAC(A)s a little later than the Marines, selecting the F-14 for the mission following the aircraft's metamorphosis into a precision bomber in the mid 1990s. The only two-seat TACAIR jet operating from a carrier deck that possessed the range, speed, targeting equipment, avionics and radios capable of performing this highly demanding mission, the Tomcat made its FAC(A) combat debut over Kosovo in Operation *Allied Force* in March 1999. The leading role played by US naval aviation in OEF two years later saw the Tomcat FAC(A) concept prove its worth over and over again.

Lessons learned in this campaign had been worked into the FAC(A) training syllabus conducted by NSAWC and the Strike Fighter Weapons School Atlantic at Fallon and El Centro, and the Hornet units operating with CTF-50/60 planned to make full use of their air wings' FAC(A) crews in OIF.

The F-14 crews really earned their flight pay when myriad Hornet pilots, typically running low on fuel, were desperately trying to acquire and prosecute targets either in a kill box or during a CAS mission. There would be plenty of jets ready to drop their bombs, but a shortage of real targets amongst all the potential contacts that needed to be attacked. It was therefore up to the FAC(A)s to work out what were the bona fide targets by talking over the radio with SOF teams on the ground, liaising with airborne controllers and scouring enemy territory with their own target sensors.

It was while controlling the airspace over open kill boxes as part of the Tomcat's Strike Coordination And Reconnaissance (SCAR) and FAC(A) missions that the jet's two-man crew excelled. A big part of the FAC(A) tasking is situational awareness, which comes with experience, and all of the FAC(A)-qualified crews in OIF had this in abundance.

Lt Cdr Blackwelder of VFA-105 regularly worked with VF-32 during the northern campaign, the Tomcat squadron buddy-lasing about 35 per cent of the 416 LGBs dropped by CVW-3's trio of Hornet units in OIF. He recalled;

'The Tomcat had 20,000 lbs of gas and we had 14,000 lbs. That gave the VF-32 crews about 15 minutes more loiter time over the target than we had – they could stretch this to 20 minutes by "hanging on their blades". They needed every minute of this for their FAC(A) mission, as they had to have their eyes firmly locked on the target to allow us to concentrate on simply running in and getting our LGB guided onto the aim point by them, using their LANTIRN pod. We had to get our ordnance off in a timely fashion and then depart due to our limited fuel.'

Squadronmate Lt Mike Kraus also benefited from VF-32's FAC(A) skills;

'I worked four times with the Tomcats, VF-32 either lasing or providing the FAC(A) control. In either role, the F-14 crew would have gone into the area first and been given a situation report by the ground FAC. The SOF guys would then pass control of the targeting for the strikers over to the Tomcat crew. The latter would in turn be getting target hit assessments from the FAC after every Hornet bombing run.

'Where the Tomcat crews really helped us out was by relaying target information in quick time. Typically, we would only have sufficient fuel aboard to loiter on-station over the target area for 15 minutes at most, and it could take the ground FACs a good chunk of that time to give us all the relevant information on any threats in the area, the target itself, and how best to attack it. While all this was going on, you always had one eye on your watch, as you knew that there was another section of Hornets coming in behind yours, and your gas would be getting to a critical state in less than 15 minutes.

'The Tomcat FAC(A) crew would usually arrive over the target while you were still on the tanker, get all the up-to-date information from the SOF FAC and then turn this into "naval aviator talk", thus allowing you to simply cycle through the area, drop your bombs with the minimum of fuss and leave.

'The FAC(A) missions did not always go to plan, however, and I feel that the Tomcat crews were perhaps not as prepared as they should have been for some of the more challenging targets that we were given up north. For example, I was once told upon arriving on station that I was to bomb a bunker, and I looked down and saw 40 bunkers! I asked the FAC(A) crew which one I was supposed to hit, and they then spent the next few minutes arguing between themselves about which bunker I should bomb.'

Although the presence of FAC(A)s usually sped up the bombing process for Hornet crews conducting CAS sorties, mission duration still remained long throughout OIF, as VFA-105 CO Cdr Lalor recounted;

'Most OIF sorties were lengthy and the pace was gruelling. Missions lasted between five and seven hours' flight time on average. The two

Right
Lot XIII F/A-18C BuNo 164246 'Canyon 410' overflies Saddam Dam in mid April 2003. Renamed Mosul Dam for the nearby city post-war, this massive complex also boasts a hydroelectric power station. Potential targets such as this were removed from the ATO in the weeks leading up to OIF, as CENTCOM senior commanders realised that these sites would be crucial in allowing Iraq to function normally post-war. The enemy also realised this within days of the conflict commencing, as VFA-15's Cdr Ed Langford recalled;
'There was an enemy spotter who sat atop Saddam Dam with a pair of NVGs, and he would tip off troops in the area that we were coming. There was nothing we could do to stop him from the air, as we did not want to ruin the infrastructure of the country by taking out the dam. We just had to "suck it up". Every time we went into Iraq the enemy knew that we were coming, and they would start shooting at us'
(Lt Bobby Baker)

KC-135R 59-1508 of the 92nd ARW's 97th ARS pumps fuel into 'Canyon 402' (Lot XIII F/A-18C BuNo 164236) while VF-32's 'Gypsy 101' (F-14B BuNo 161860) holds station off the tanker's right wing. Both jets are armed with GBU-12s
(Cdr Tom Lalor)

carriers worked shifts on a 12 hours on, 12 hours off basis, and although "HST" was the day carrier, we were usually kept up most of the night mission planning. We would get our tasking from the CAOC at about 2200 hrs and then have about six hours to put together a mission plan. By about 0400 hrs it was time to brief the flight. We would launch at sunrise and return to the carrier at about lunchtime. After our mission debriefs, we would grab a quick bite to eat followed by some sleep, before doing it all over again. This went on non-stop for 26 days without a day off.

'To keep up with the pace, the flight surgeons issued us with "stop" and "go" pills, as we called them. The "stop" pills provided a restful six hours of sleep and left us feeling refreshed afterwards. The pills were crucial because without them the adrenalin rush from combat made it very difficult to get any quality rest. Conversely, once safely off target and out of harm's way, it sometimes became hard to stay alert for the long trip back to the ship. That's where the "go" pills helped out. I would take one about 45 minutes before touchdown so as to have all of my mental faculties in top order for the arrested landing on the carrier deck.

'After about two weeks of OIF, we had all flown our monthly limit of 80 hours, which meant that we had to get a special waiver from the ship's flight surgeons to continue.

'The F/A-18 has never been known for its comfortable ejection seat. With my apologies to Martin-Baker (the British manufacturers of the Hornet's SJU-5/A ejection seat), it is not much better than sitting on a wooden bench. Spending six hours a day crammed into the jet's snug little cockpit, strapped tightly into a seat that was designed for one-hour flights, made for some awfully sore backsides before very long. After a few days, I would man up my aircraft and lower myself gingerly into the seat, dreading the six hours of discomfort that lay ahead.

'While transiting to and from the tanker rendezvous, we would loosen

Below
Like all other Hornet units in CTF-60, VFA-105 operated its jets in 'hard wing' configuration throughout OIF. This aircraft is carrying wingtip-mounted AIM-9Ms, a fuselage-mounted AIM-120C, two GBU-12s and a single GBU-32 (*Cdr Tom Lalor*)

our lap belt straps and lift ourselves up off of our so-called "cushions" to get the blood flowing again. While it can't begin to compare to the levels of discomfort endured by the poor infantry soldier sleeping in a cold, wet foxhole, I won't soon forget just how physically tiring the early pace of OIF was.'

The naval aviators aboard CVN-71 had it just as hard, with the added 'thrill' of a night recovery thrown into the mix. Lt Cdr Metzger of VFA-15 recalled;

'The mission duration did not decrease a whole lot once we were

gained access to Turkish airspace, with most sorties lasting between five and seven hours, and the number of times you aerial refuelled in the Hornet being reduced to three. The transit time to Iraq was indeed shorter, but we now spent much longer over the target area performing CAS. On our very first mission of the war, we basically took off, tanked, whacked our assigned target on the first pass and left. For our missions from Op Area One, we would actually be on station waiting for tasking. The shortest mission I flew in the war lasted three-and-a-half hours. I basically took off, tanked, got in country, dropped my ordnance soon after arriving on station and then left. Most were appreciably longer.

'These missions took a toll on your body, with your lower extremities – legs and feet – taking a real pounding, as you really cannot move them too much in the confines of the cockpit. Upon returning to the carrier and shutting down, I would have to sit in the jet for a short while and then slowly stand up in the cockpit before climbing out, as my legs did not work too well straight away.

'The NVGs also inflicted their own damage too. They clipped onto your helmet, and were held in place by your mask, with the bottom of the NVGs resting on your nose. By the last week of the war the bridge of my

Cdr Tom Lalor snapped this self-portrait, with his wingman in 'Canyon 412' (Lot XIII F/A-18C BuNo 164215) closed up alongside him, in early April 2003. Again, LGBs can be seen beneath the wings of the 'Dash Two' jet (*Cdr Tom Lalor*)

Bombs gone, 'Canyon 404' (Lot XIII F/A-18C BuNo 164244) returns to CVN-75 after one of its last missions of OIF. The aircraft's bomb log to the left of its '404' modex features a mix of LGB and JDAM symbols (*Cdr Tom Lalor*)

nose was raw from where the NVGs had rubbed on it continuously for up to seven hours at a time. Just putting the mask on was painful during that final week of OIF.

'We had to wear the NVGs, though, in order to carry out our mission as the night air wing. Anything that was lit could be readily seen with them, and they gave us 20/40 vision. We had a real advantage when flying around Kirkuk, as the city was literally surrounded by oilfields, and the burning vents from these would light the nearby ridgeline for us. The combination of the vents and the NVGs allowed us to see the ground if the weather was clear – which it rarely was.

'Aside from my chafed nose and stiff legs, I also suffered from numb heels for weeks after the war had finished. This was caused by my lack of feet movement for hours on end in the cockpit.'

RISK TAKING

The weather over northern Iraq slowly began to improve in the wake of the Bashur landings on 26/27 March, and for the next ten days CTF-60 made up for lost time by flying a sustained campaign of CAS for SOF teams as they fanned out across northern Iraq. Aside from delivering JDAM and LGBs, several Hornet units also went that extra mile in providing fire support by strafing Iraqi positions when requested by the FACs that they were working with.

One of the first to fire his 20 mm cannon in action was Lt Cdr Blackwelder from VFA-105, who explained to the author how his actions subsequently caused some soul searching amongst CTF-60 staffers aboard CVN-75;

'Early on in the conflict I think that all naval aviators had gone into action with a "knife in the teeth" kind of mindset, with a certain degree of risk being tolerated in order to get the war won. However, this quickly changed when the invasion from the north was cancelled. We no longer had the situation where 65,000 of our guys were in life-threatening close contact with the Iraqi Republican Guard.

'The northern campaign took on a completely different complexion when it became obvious that there would be no invasion. The CTF-60 admiral clearly decided early on into the war that he did not want to take unnecessary risks with his aircrews – he felt that losing a jet taking out a couple of Iraqi soldiers in a pick-up truck was not a fair exchange. Therefore, the level of allowable risk was raised within two or three days of OIF commencing.

'On my first fair weather mission of the war, my wingman, Lt Michael Amos, and I had been dropping LGBs on a military complex when the FAC asked us to strafe the target. I am not as good a gunner as Michael, who ripped the hell out of one of the buildings we fired on. I was fully aware that our strafing runs, which bottomed out at between 2000 ft and 5000 ft, placed us well inside the infrared missile threat zone, and on my long flight back to the ship I began to wonder whether I should have agreed to make those passes, and whether they had really helped the cause much. Nonetheless, I felt more alive during the course of those strafing runs than I did at any other point in the whole campaign.

'Despite being told to reduce the level of risk we were exposing ourselves to, we had had no direct guidance on what we could and couldn't do, and that included strafing. I think we surprised a few people on the ship when we told them what we had just done. Once our target video footage had been analysed by CVW-3, CAG and the CTF-60 staffers told the fast jet guys to think twice about strafing because of the increased IADS risk that we faced the closer we got to the ground.'

Despite the TACAIR crews in CVW-3 being fully cognisant of the risks associated with strafing, VF-32 and the three Hornet squadrons aboard CVN-75 still got through their fair share of 20 mm ammunition – 1128 rounds were fired by the F-14s and no fewer than 16,285 by the F/A-18s. As the night air wing, CVW-8 did very little strafing by comparison. Indeed, only VFA-87 and VFA-201 used the cannon in combat, firing 1218 rounds between them during early dawn missions.

Lt Mike Kraus of VFA-105 remembered that the strafing criteria applied by pilots to the FACs' requests for gunnery passes became more critical as the conflict progressed;

'The SOF guys were very good at hiding themselves, so there really was no need to go strafing targets in order to protect them as most of the time the Iraqis had no idea where our FACs were. There was a transition from the early missions in OIF, when FACs would call us down to strafe despite not being in contact with the Iraqis, to us quizzing them as to their status in respect to the enemy. We would ask them "Are you in close contact with the enemy, and do they know that you are there?" If they replied that they could see the Iraqis, but that the enemy could not see them, we would tell them "Let's keep this nice and safe here because no one is going to get hurt if we don't come down and strafe unnecessarily".

'However, if you could hear the SOF guys engaging the enemy with small arms fire over the radio, then you would go down and do whatever you could for them to make sure that the FAC did not get into further trouble.

'Our selective policy on strafing came about due to our observance of a higher level of caution as requested by CAG and the admiral within days of OIF kicking off.'

Despite the less than enthusiastic response to his first strafing episode by his seniors in CVW-3, Lt Cdr

Reservist maintainers from VFA-201 use a SHOLS to help winch a recently serviced M61A1 Vulcan cannon back into the nose of 'Hunter 207' (Lot VIII F/A-18A+ BuNo 162899). This delicate operation is taking place in the hangar bay of CVN-71 after the aircraft had partaken in a rare CVW-8 strafing attack during OIF. VFA-201 fired just 477 rounds in anger during the war, VFA-87 741 rounds and VFA-15 none at all – VF-213 did not strafe either. The Hornet's gun metal grey ammunition drum holds 578 rounds in total (*PH1 James Foehl*)

Blackwelder 'went for his gun' again several days later when supporting a SOF FAC who had literally been forced to run for his life;

'There was a guy camped out southeast of Bashur who operated with the call-sign of "Echo-Tango". The first time I worked with him he was taking fire, and you could hear him on the radio huffing and puffing as he was running away from the enemy whilst simultaneously talking to me! He was telling me "They're moving up the road and coming in on me". We raced in and did some good strafing work, which allowed the SOF guy to escape. I felt great after this mission because I knew that we had just helped out a buddy on the ground. You would have thought that after this close shave "Echo-Tango" would have cleared out of the area, but for the next week he seemed to be doing the same thing nearly every day!'

ANATOMY OF A FAC MISSION

Although every mission was different for TACAIR crews in respect to the target(s) being hit, the geographical location of the aim points, weather conditions and the weapon(s) employed, a typical northern front CAS sortie would be run as follows. Instead of a dedicated mission lead, the departing jets would have a package commander who would brief everybody participating in the flight aboard the carrier prior to launching. The package commander would give the crews an up-to-date weather report, the location of the tanker support, what radio frequencies were being used and the predicted IADS threat.

A typical package of eight to ten jets (two or four Tomcats and six or eight Hornets, with perhaps a single Prowler along to supply dedicated SEAD support) would launch from the carrier and head southeast over Turkey, rendezvousing with a KC-135 or KC-10 tanker near the border with Iraq. With their tanks topped off, the jets would break up into two-aircraft elements, and the element lead would then call up the E-2 controller and tell him that they were ready for mission tasking. The lead

An unidentified pilot from VFA-37 walks to his Hornet aboard CVN-75, thus signalling the start of yet another mission
(*PH1 Michael W Pendergrass*)

A section of LGB-toting VFA-37 jets refuel in unison from 97th ARS/92nd ARW KC-135R 59-1508 (*VFA-37*)

pilot would let the controller know what type of aircraft they were flying, what ordnance they were carrying and their fuel state. They would then be given a tasking, which usually consisted of location coordinates and a frequency for their dedicated ground FAC, or the coordinates for a kill box should there be no FACs available.

Pushing into northern Iraq as a section of two jets or occasionally as a division of four, the strike lead would head towards the ground FAC's location and then attempt to raise him on the radio. In most cases, the SOF FACs were using hand-held radios, and the receiving aircraft needed to be virtually overhead their position to talk to them, particularly when they were working in the mountains east of Mosul and Kirkuk. Realising that the Hornets, in particular, had only limited time on station, the FACs usually had tasking for CTF-60 jets right away, so they were ready to accept ordnance as soon as the crews checked in.

In order to expedite the attack phase of the mission, the FAC and the pilot would communicate with each other via a 9-line attack brief. This was short, clipped and concise, with the SOF FACs being 'big on comms brevity', as one F-14 OIF veteran recalled. Pilots were left with the impression that the guys on the ground did not want to talk on the radio for any extended period of time.

The 9-line attack brief is the key element in effective CAS, and it needs to contain all of the information required by the pilot to ingress, conduct the attack and egress. The components of the brief are as follows;

1) Initial Point (IP) – location from where CAS jet begins attack run

2) Bearing/offset – bearing IP to target, offset direction (left/right)

3) Distance – distance to target from IP in nautical miles for jets

4) Elevation – elevation of target in feet/metres above Mean Sea Level

5) Target Description

6) Target Location – coordinates for target

7) Mark – type of visual or laser/IR mark that FAC puts on/near target

8) Friendlies – bearing and distance from target to nearest friendly unit (not coordinates to minimise confusion with target coordinates)

9) Egress – direction and IP for the CAS aircraft to fly after attacking the target in order to clear the target area.

Additional information was provided after the 9-line brief, including the expected Time-on-Target (time when CAS aircraft's bombs must hit the target) and Final Attack Heading/Cone (either a heading or an arc of headings that the CAS aircraft must fly down when delivering weapons onto the target). This information would be relayed to the pilot via a radio frequency unique to this particular FAC team, the latter having literally a phonebook of frequencies that they could choose from – the teams switched these on a daily basis. Each FAC team had at least two radios, and these all needed to have unique frequencies.

The pilots in turn had a notebook-sized frequency 'smart pack' that they would leaf through in order to ascertain the correct channel to dial into their radios to allow them to communicate securely with their FAC. Aside from the frequency tables, the pack also contained a procedural listing for all the main aspects of a typical combat mission in OIF. Hornet pilots quickly customised their packs, highlighting, tabbing and laminating throughout so as to allow the relevant pages to be quickly referenced when on tasking.

CVW-8 CAG Capt David Newland was not a fan of the way the radio communications aspect of OIF was structured;

'I had great sympathy for my Hornet pilots who had to handle the CAS/FAC deal at night on their own. The whole OIF set up was run in typical Air Force fashion, which meant that it turned into a real "comms grill". You had to talk to the AWACS first, then switch to an overall tanking frequency, then change to your specific tanker frequency. Once in country, you had to communicate on yet another frequency to the "big picture" guy in the AWACS or the E-2, who in turn switched the comms to your particular mission frequency, before giving you yet another frequency on which your FAC was operating!

'In order to cope with this, we always had to fly with a notebook an inch thick that contained all of our coded frequencies listed by colour. Typically, we would get instructions in code from the AWACS such as "tune to 'Purple 6'" or "go to 'Mauve 18'". We would then flick through the book, find the relevant code and dial it into our radio. Some of the frequencies were of course on the secure *Have Quick* system, and that took even more flipping around on the radio in order to talk to your tanker, AWACS controller or FAC!'

The limited range of the ground FACs' hand-held radios also caused problems, as they could not talk to the AWACS controller at all because the latter was too far away, circling over Turkey. Instead, they had to converse through another agency equipped with more powerful radios, which would in turn contact the AWACS to inform them that they had tasking in-theatre. Pilots would then be passed this information, along with the FAC's frequency, and they would talk directly with the controller on the ground. The pilot would physically write down the FAC's 9-line brief onto his kneeboard, and he would then read back the coordinates to check that he had copied them correctly. The FAC would confirm with a simple 'Yes', or a mike click. Once he had received this, the pilot would then start to punch the target coordinates into the bomb guidance system.

With all the targeting parameters confirmed, the pilot then started working out how best to attack the target. Typically, an attack would be structured in a 'textbook' way, pilots having briefed for just this type of mission back on the ship. They would tailor their general tactics to suit the situation at hand, confident in the knowledge that they had sound training techniques to fall back on should the target prove difficult to hit.

Once the release parameters had been met, the pilot would tell the FAC that he was set up for his run in to the target, giving him the 'Wings Level' call, which would prompt his reply of 'Cleared Hot'. The pilot now had the FAC's authority to release his ordnance – the former could not do so without the latter's approval. Once the FAC had declared the target 'hostile', the pilot was happy to drop his bombs. The FAC's view of the enemy forces was usually far better than the pilot's, so the final call on whether to release the ordnance or not was ultimately his to make. A pilot would never question his decision.

With the Hornet set up correctly and the target locked up either by the NITE Hawk FLIR pod or the FAC's hand-held Viper laser designator, the weapon's release symbology in the HUD, combined with an aural tone in the cockpit, told the pilot exactly when it had automatically

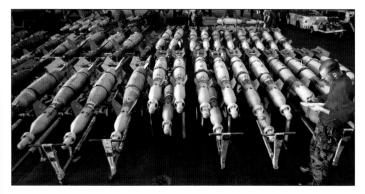

LGBs dominate the hangar deck of CVN-75 in early April 2003. The weapons on the right, loaded three per skid, are 500-lb GBU-12s, the larger bombs in the foreground to the left are 1000-lb GBU-16s and the trio of big-finned LGBs in the back row are 2000-lb GBU-24s. CVW-3's trio of Hornet units dropped 366 GBU-12s and 50 GBU-16s in OIF, but no GBU-24s (*via VFA-105*)

Yet another LGB is released over northern Iraq during OIF, this time from the outer starboard wing pylon of a VFA-37 jet. Note how the pilot has placed his Hornet in a shallow dive during his bombing run (*Lt Geoff Bowman*)

released either the JDAM or the LGB. Simultaneously, the pilot also hit the bomb release button on top of the Hands On Throttle And Stick (HOTAS) just to make sure that the ordnance left his jet at the optimum time.

As previously mentioned in this chapter, radio communication was the key element in achieving a satisfactory, and expeditious, outcome to a FAC-controlled mission in OIF. Ironically, in the north, radios were also the weakest link in the technology chain, as VFA-87's Cdr Greg Fenton explained;

'The FACs were limited by the power of the batteries in their radios, which meant that they could only transmit over a certain range. We still had to talk to them when flying a CAS mission, however, as according to our rules of engagement we had to be in direct contact with the FAC before we were allowed to drop any ordnance. Now, if you were striking a back-up target in a kill box or attacking a TST, then you would receive location coordinates from an E-2 controller, who had the authority to clear us to drop our bombs. We experienced no communication problems when speaking with our dedicated AWACS platforms.

'Communication between the pilot and the FAC could be difficult at times, especially if the frequencies weren't quite right or the SOF guy had a weak radio or low battery power. On some occasions you could only hear him when you were right on top of him. We frequently struggled to recognise the coordinates when first relayed, but by us reading them back to the FAC two or three times, we quickly straightened out where the target was. By adhering rigidly to this "read back" procedure, VFA-87 had no blue-on-blue episodes, or errors in bomb dropping.'

VFA-15 CO Cdr Andy Lewis was also less than impressed with the radio 'comms' that he experienced in OIF;

'Communication with the FAC was usually via our KY-58 secure radio, which is akin to talking with your head in a trash can. The CAS was normally the talk-on type, with the collateral damage onus falling

squarely on the shoulders of the aircrew. Occasionally we would drop on the first pass, but most of the time we needed to make a couple of runs to ensure positive target identification and deconfliction. On most sorties, we would make another trip (or two) back to the tankers until our Vulnerability Window expired. After we ran out of time and/or ordnance, we would return to the ship for the night recovery.

'Having operational experience in *Desert Storm* and *Deny Flight* as a Junior Officer, OEF as the XO of

The pilot of 'Canyon 400' (Lot XIII
F/A-18C BuNo 164200) retracts his
refuelling probe after topping off
his fuel from an unidentified USAF
tanker. The Hornet is armed with
two 500-lb GBU-12s and a single
AGM-154A JSOW. By war's end this
particular aircraft was VFA-105's
leading JSOW dropper, its pilots
having expended four AGM-154As.
Eleven LGB and two JDAM symbols
completed the jet's scoreboard,
making it the unit's leading bomber
(via Lt Col Mark Hasara)

Bathed in early evening light,
'Valion 312' cruises over solid cloud
at dusk as part of the first night
package from CVN-71. Jets
launched from 'TR' at the start
of the vessel's night shift usually
departed at dusk (Lt(jg) Jon Biehl)

VFA-15 and several bouts of *Southern Watch*, I can honestly say that OIF consistently threw up the toughest conditions in which to be successful and deliver ordnance on target.'

Aside from radio communication, weather was the other big factor that influenced just how well the prosecution of CAS targets went in the north, as Lt Cdr Blackwelder recalled;

'The weather in this region was far from predictable at this time of year, and it was always good to have someone in-country telling you what the conditions were like in the area where you had been tasked with working, or if you were going to be able to work at all. Once airborne, we would try and raise any squadronmates who were coming back north off station in order to get an up-to-the-minute weather report. If you knew that the whole of western Iraq was socked in, or covered in layered cloud, you could then start working out just how much of a risk you were prepared to take to prosecute your target.

'When the weather was clear, it was simply a matter of getting your gas, leaving the tanker and then talking to your AWACS controller, who would then give you the location and frequency of your FAC guy. By the

time you had entered the waypoint and coordinates in the jet's navigation computer, you had covered another 25 miles, and by the time you started talking with the FAC on the ground you were pretty much right over his position.

'It was not uncommon to come off the tanker, make contact with a FAC and then spend the entire bag of gas trying to figure out exactly what he was talking about! He would tell you to drop your bomb, and seconds later he would say, "Okay, I heard that one, but I didn't see it". I would reply, "I guess I'm not in the right area then. Let me go back and get some more gas and then we can try this again". Pilots would often have to make a couple of trips to the tanker before they finally figured out what targets their FAC was trying to get them to drop their ordnance on!

'In a lot of cases, you had to get a bomb on the ground before the FAC could talk you onto the target he wanted hit. Sometimes that didn't help, however. The difficulty for us was converting the FAC's instructions that we were so many feet or metres away from the target when we were bombing from a height of anywhere between 15,000 ft and 35,000 ft. He would typically tell us "we were this far away from the target", and I would reply "I see this road and this road. Was it that far away, or half of that distance?" If you were close with your first drop, then further instructions from the FAC would help, but if you were 300 ft or more away then further guidance was of little use.'

The actual whereabouts of the FACs themselves in relation to the targets that they wanted hit could also prove problematic for the Hornet pilots. Fratricide was to be avoided at all costs, and TACAIR crews were adamant that they would not hit aim points if they were unable to pinpoint the position of their FAC prior to releasing their ordnance. CVW-3 DCAG Capt Pat Rainey was one of those pilots who turned down a target because he was unsure of where the friendlies were;

'About four or five days before the end of the war, we were flying around Tikrit with JDAM-equipped jets looking for a weapons depot. We got the word from our controller that a FAC team needed us in the northeastern sector of the country. The SOF guys had inserted a FAC team near a 60-mile stretch of road that came out of Baghdad and headed east into Iran. These guys were doing some excellent work cutting off convoys trying to get out of Iraq.

'The weather was bad in the Mosul-Kirkuk-Tikrit-Baghdad "horseshoe", but up on the border with Iran it was all clear. We came racing down the eastern side of Iraq to Baghdad after getting gas, and then spent 20 minutes looking for the FAC team. Usually, you could spot the FAC team, or you at least knew where they were so that you were happy to drop your bombs without the risk of fratricide. With these guys, we never did manage to pinpoint their location, and then they told us that they were on motorcycles! I radioed the FACs and informed them that although we would like to help, I was not comfortable enough with their position in order to drop my bombs.'

FOREIGN FACs

CAS missions were not exclusively controlled by American FACs in the north, despite JSOTF-N primarily consisting of SOF personnel drawn from the US Army's 10th Special Forces Group (Airborne). Lt Cdr

Norman Metzger worked with FAC teams from Britain and Australia, as well as the US;

'One area where this conflict differed greatly from previous campaigns that I had been involved in was the fact that were receiving FAC control from SOF guys that had been drawn from the British and Australian SAS, rather than just our own Navy SEALs or Army and Marine FACs. They are not the same animal, whether that be in the type of communications equipment they use or the procedures they adopt. We understood how our guys operated in the field, but the SAS did things rather differently.

'For example, it was not unusual for them to identify a target for us and then leave, telling us later if we had hit it or not. Our guys would usually remain in the area and let us know straight away if we had hit the aim point, and if we had missed, they would tell us what we needed to do to make sure that the target or threat went away. The SAS style of operations was not the CAS that I was used to doing.

'However, on some occasions you did not have to worry about accidentally hitting the good guys because there were vast areas of northern Iraq that were free of Coalition forces. Pre-war, we had spent a lot of time working on our ability to locate our guys on the ground in relation to where the target was, as we expected to be operating along the forward edge of a battlefield as they did down south. In OIF in the north, we did not have that kind of problem. Indeed, collateral damage issues were nowhere near as big a deal as they could have been had a full-scale invasion taken place. This allowed us to hit a number of Iraqi ammunition storage areas without having to worry about the effects of secondary explosions on the immediate area around the target.'

Squadronmate Cdr Ed Langford also found that working with Coalition forces could be a real challenge, especially as the conflict progressed and Iraqi towns and cities in the north began to fall to US-backed Kurdish Peshmerga fighters;

'On our front, we often did not know "who was who in the zoo", and where exactly they were on the ground, from one day to the next. You had the Kurds, and their different factions, our own regular Army forces and SOF teams and the British and Australian SAS. We often struggled to work out who was good and who was bad, which of course provided us with one of our biggest challenges in the north. Things only got worse as the war progressed, for Kurdish freedom fighters started to use abandoned Iraqi tanks against their fleeing enemies! We relied on real time intelligence from FACs on the ground to prevent us from attacking such "targets", as we had no up-to-the-minute information on this back on the boat.

'The battlefield was so dynamic in the north towards the end of the war that the updated charts that we flew with, marked with the theoretical position of the frontline as of the previous mission, were effectively redundant by the time we arrived in Iraq! We basically relied on our knowledge of major road intersections – they did not move – and then got the FACs to guide us to targets in relation to where they were.'

CVW-3's DCAG Capt Pat Rainey also worked with SAS FACs very early on in the war;

'My only experience of working with our Coalition partners took the form of FAC calls from Australian SAS teams in northwestern Iraq. We detected an accent on the radio, and we asked where they were from. They had two teams in-country, working northwest of Mosul up near Saddam Dam. The Aussies were there for about two weeks, after which I am not sure what happened to them. The SOF guys would turn up under the cover of darkness and leave the same way!'

Capt Rainey also explained to the author how the results of a CAS mission were directly proportional to the type of control the pilot got from the FACs on the ground;

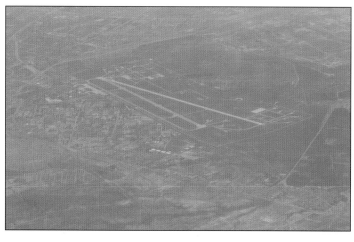

'We soon found that the success of the CAS sorties that we flew varied depending on the experience of the FAC with whom we were operating. Perhaps the best of the bunch that I worked with controlled a stretch of the main highway that ran north-south from Kirkuk to Baghdad. He had managed to get himself positioned between the road, a nearby ridgeline and Kirkuk itself. Wedged up in the hills, he had a fantastic view of the highway in both directions, as well as buildings on the outskirts of the city. The FAC's elevated vantage point also meant that he was hidden from view of the Iraqi troop convoys that were moving up and down the road.

'By the time I arrived overhead his position soon after noon, the FAC had already done some pretty impressive work that morning controlling other Hornet and Tomcat sections from CVW-3. He called my wingman (Lt Tom Heck from VFA-105) and I down, and he was literally picking out buildings, tanks and Iraqi troop concentrations for us with little difficulty at all. His control was pretty phenomenal, and he gave us some coordinates that allowed us to get our FLIR onto a headquarters building that he wanted destroyed. We duly put two LGBs into it.

'Following the detonation of our bombs, the surviving staff members in the building ran out, jumped into waiting cars and drove about half-a-mile down the road into an L-shaped shack that looked like an old gas station. I came in and put my remaining weapon into the "crotch" of the building, which in turn went "high order" – it was an ammunition depot. There were huge secondaries. Lt Heck then placed his LGB into a nearby

The dual runways of Kirkuk air base are clearly visible in this hazy view, taken by Lt Bobby Baker soon after hostilities had ended in northern Iraq. Located barely a mile from the centre of the city itself, and with the Kirkuk oil fields, refinery and petrochemical plant nearby, this airfield was one of the Operation *Super-Base* sites developed by Yugoslav contractors in the early 1980s. Boasting 24 hardened aircraft shelters, the base had support facilities for at least two fighter squadrons. It is presently home to the USAF's 506th Air Expeditionary Group (*Lt Bobby Baker*)

The pilot of 'Canyon 412' enjoys a little sight-seeing over Turkey as he heads for northern Iraq on 10 April 2003 (*Lt Bobby Baker*)

'Canyon 404' patrols over northern Iraq on the very day that Tikrit fell and CVW-3 dropped its final bombs of OIF – 14 April 2003. The aircraft returned to the carrier with its LGBs still bolted to their pylons, the Hornet ending the campaign with 13 bomb symbols to the right of its '404' modex (*Cdr Tom Lalor*)

'Bull 306' (Lot XVIII F/A-18C BuNo 165184) goes in search of a target after taking on fuel from a KC-135R of the California Air National Guard's 196th ARS/163rd ARW over a patchwork Iraqi landscape on 11 April 2003. VFA-37 achieved an outstanding 100 per cent combat sortie completion rate with its 12 jets in OIF, flying 1271 hours during 297 sorties to deliver 144 tons of air-to-ground ordnance and 9400 rounds of 20 mm ammunition (*Paul Farley*)

fuel storage facility, thinking that it was empty, and the resulting explosion was even bigger!'

Although the LGB was the preferred weapon of choice for FAC-controlled precision attacks in OIF, occasionally Hornet crews could only use JDAM because of solid cloud cover over the target areas. CAS missions still had to be flown in spite of the weather, and the J-weapons proved to be the perfect substitute for LGBs when the latter were effectively grounded by obscuration over northern Iraq. Cdr Fenton of VFA-87 employed 1000-lb JDAM on a CAS mission in early April;

'I was leading an eight-jet strike mission that consisted of Hornets and Tomcats armed exclusively with JDAM because of the poor weather that had been forecast for northern Iraq. After leaving CVN-71, we had to climb to well above 30,000 ft just to get on top of the cloud in order to fly into Iraqi airspace. The weather made tanking very difficult too, with the KC-135s spaced out between cloud layers. Finding them at night between cloud layers using radar and NVGs was a challenge in itself. Such weather conditions also created severe turbulence, making it difficult for the pilot to plug into the basket and then remain connected.

'Nevertheless, we managed to get topped off and were then directed down to our station in northern Iraq, where we were instructed by our E-2 controller to check in with a FAC. He came up on the radio moments later and told us that his SOF team was being engaged by Iraqi forces.

'At night, it is difficult to get a feel for what troops mean by "engaged". Was someone lobbing mortar shells at them, or attacking them with small arms fire? I never did find this out, although post-mission feedback indicated that we had attacked troops firing mortars and howitzers from a fortified emplacement.

'Despite being engaged, the FAC wasted no time in passing us coordinates for a target that he needed taking down. Although an LGB would have been better suited to this type of target, the weapon's seeker head would have been unable to pick up the FLIR pod's laser designating spot on the emplacement due to the solid cloud cover. Simply put, the bomb would not have guided with any accuracy.

'The FAC was confident that his target coordinates were sound, so we simply punched the numbers into the jet's weapons system and declared that we were ready to drop. We verified the coordinates with the FAC to ensure that we had not inputted incorrect data into the GPS system, and once this process was completed, he set up a run-in for us that deconflicted our weapons from his position. The FAC then cleared us to release our ordnance, and the GPS guided the bombs through the various layers of cloud between us and the ground for a direct hit on the target. The attack was apparently successful, for the FAC quickly got on the radio and said that he had no more use for us. The mortar or artillery fire that he was observing had ceased.

'Operating with JDAM in the CAS mission is vastly different to how I was trained to fly close air support. My training involved talking to the FAC directly, visually "eyeballing" the target and then rolling in and diving on it with a dumb bomb. With today's GPS weapons, you can stand off and drop your bombs through the clouds. The biggest issue with the new bombs is verifying that you are dropping in an area clear of friendly forces.'

The versatility of the new-generation J-weapons such as JDAM and JSOW greatly expanded the multi-role capabilities of the F/A-18 in OIF, as Lt Cdr Metzger discovered for himself over Tikrit towards the end of the campaign;

'Whilst in the process of forming up a 12-jet standard on-call CAS package after launching from CVN-71, my wingman experienced problems off the catapult stroke and had to abort. We always had spares ready for every event in case something like this occurred, so Lt Cdr Koss from VFA-87 was launched to join the formation. I was configured with a JSOW and a HARM and he was carrying a JDAM and two LGBs.

'Over the next three hours, the two of us shot and/or dropped literally every piece of ordnance that was expended from a Hornet during OIF! We bombed two trucks loaded with munitions, the HARM took out an SA-2 site and the JSOW destroyed a target near Tikrit, although we were too far away to see exactly what the latter was, of course. We received tasking for all of these targets when we were on station in Iraq.

'Our ability to provide CAS support and hit other targets such as SAM sites on the same mission was perfectly illustrated during this sortie. I launched my HARM in support of someone else in my group who needed protection from SAM threats whilst delivering his bombs. At the same time, other jets in my strike package were jamming Iraqi radar sites and bombing targets, and all of this was being coordinated through the AWACS controllers and the FACs in real time – none of the targets that we hit were pre-planned. Indeed, the planning on the ship prior to missions like this consisted primarily of making sure that all of our frequencies deconflicted with those being used by other formations in-theatre at the same time.

'We got some exposure to these real time missions during our pre-cruise work-ups, and I for one was very glad that we had had the opportunity to do this in a training environment so that everyone was "on the same page" by the time we got to fly in OIF.

'This particular mission is a perfect example of what the F/A-18 strike fighter is all about. We spend all of our time trying to stay on top of how all the weapons systems that can be deployed from the Hornet work, and how they integrate with the overall war plan. To have one section deliver such a wide variety of ordnance with such success is a testament to the concept of the strike fighter, and its ability to carry out tactical strikes on targets whilst still directly supporting the guys on the ground.'

BATTLE OF DEBECKA PASS

The northern campaign was witness to very few large-scale battles in the truest sense of the word during OIF simply because the SOF teams relied on stealth, rather than confrontation, to get the job done. Very occasionally, more heavily armed groups of Kurdish Peshmerga fighters would take on the Iraqi Army in their drive to capture the larger towns in the region. One such battle took place on 6 April in the Debecka Pass, which was a major route through the mountains that separated Mosul from Kirkuk. Elements of an Iraqi mechanised brigade surrounded several US SOF teams and Kurdish militiamen and threatened to overrun their position.

The Coalition forces, lacking any kind of armour or heavy artillery support, urgently called on CTF-60 to help them fend off the Iraqis. Despite typically poor weather blanketing the area, CVW-3 responded with a series of timely strikes that knocked out at least eight T-55 main battle tanks and 16 BMP-1 tracked infantry combat vehicles. One of the pilots to engage the enemy was VFA-105's Lt Bobby Baker;

'The weather on this day was absolutely horrible, with a solid cloud layer from 7000 ft to greater than 36,000 ft – my section leader, Lt Johnny Caldwell, and I actually tried to climb above it but we never managed to get on top of the cloud! We launched in the darkness just prior to sunrise and joined up overhead the ship. My section then headed east along the Turkish border into northern Iraq, where we planned to top off our fuel tanks prior to proceeding on our mission.

'Usually, we flew for hours with the sun directly in our faces as it rose in the east, but this morning was very different. With visibility of less than half-a-mile, we didn't have to worry about having the sun in our eyes. However, we would be earning our pay trying to find and then join up on a KC-135 without hitting it, hitting each other or hitting anyone else. Additionally, all of our tactical flying would be conducted in the clouds.

'Actually finding the tanker was the easy part, for once we had the KC-135 in sight, the real work began trying to calm our nerves. I then had to focus all of my attention on smoothly placing the probe into the refuelling basket while flying IMC (Instrument Meteorological Conditions) in turbulence.

'On several occasions during OIF, CTF-60 jets had to divert to airfields in Turkey and elsewhere when their probe tips were snapped off and/or the refuelling basket had broken free from the hose due to improper pilot technique and/or faulty equipment. I had been lucky up to this point in the war, and the thought of limping a jet into a foreign, unfamiliar airfield with minimum fuel onboard haunted me throughout OIF.

'The conditions on this sortie were as bad as they got during the campaign, and it wasn't until we were within 4000 ft of the KC-135 that we started seeing the strobe lights from our Air Force tanker. Once behind the four-engined jet, I watched as the basket bobbed and weaved, with oscillations reaching three to five feet at a time. We had to wait until the basket settled down and then we could literally take a stab at it. Despite the "environmentals", thanks partly to luck and partly to skill, the tanking was uneventful.

'Tanks topped off, Caldwell and I headed south and were quickly assigned to a FAC requesting air support in the vicinity of Kirkuk. Normally, our mission would have been cancelled due to the terrible weather, but our troops on the ground (in the Debecka Pass) were taking direct fire from the enemy. The AWACS told us that Iraqi tanks, wheeled vehicles and personnel were in the vicinity of a road intersection, with our SOF teams holed up nearby. The FAC sounded exhausted and scared as he requested our help on the radio. They needed air support immediately and were severely outnumbered.

'At that moment our combat training kicked into high gear, and we knew that we were going to do everything in our power to eliminate the threat and save our ground forces. We received the target coordinates from the FAC, but we were initially unable to fly below the weather without descending beneath the strictly observed theatre "hard deck" altitude limit, beneath which we were exposed to AAA and SAMs. The FAC stated that he could hear us but couldn't see us to guide us onto the targets.

'Without the ability to see the targets with our sensors or with our eyeballs, we needed a different tactic if we were to assist the FAC and eradicate the enemy threat. The SOF guys needed to provide guidance to ensure that our LGBs hit the targets of their choosing. They passed the coordinates of the tanks and we set up our formation while still in the clouds. Since we were using LGBs instead of GPS weapons, we needed to identify the target area to prevent dropping ordnance on our troops.

'With the thought of being shot down lingering in the back of my mind, Lt Caldwell led me down through the clouds until we broke out in clear air just a few thousand feet above the ground. Using our NITE Hawk target designator and ground-mapping radar, we established a

'Canyon 401' heads south towards Iraq over the snow-covered mountain peaks of Kurdistan in early April 2003. CVW-3 played a key role in preventing SOF and Kurdish forces from being overrun by Iraqi troops during a pitched battle in poor weather in terrain not too dissimilar to this during the Battle of Debecka Pass on 6 April (*Lt Bobby Baker*)

Although CTF-60 expended its last ordnance on 14 April 2003, TACAIR assets continued to patrol over Iraq fully bombed up just in case Coalition troops on the ground encountered pockets of resistance. Here, 'Bull 302' returns to CVN-75 with its weapons still aboard in late April 2003. VFA-87 XO Cdr Greg Fenton explained to the author that the Hornet can be a bit of a handful in this configuration around the boat;

'Recovering aboard ship with unexpended ordnance is always a big issue for us in the legacy Hornet. Early on in OIF, we launched with the heavier 2000-lb JDAM as we figured that it was going to be dropped. Therefore, in the first two weeks of the war we employed the GBU-31s a lot. On my missions, flown later in the conflict, I only dropped a single 2000-lb JDAM and a slew of 1000-lb GBU-32/35s. Our load-out in the final week of the war, when we weren't sure whether we would be dropping our bombs or not, was typically a 1000-lb JDAM and a 500-lb LGB. Such a configuration was easily brought back aboard the ship' (VFA-37)

lead-trail formation as we ran in on the tanks.

'Lt Caldwell released his 1000-lb GBU-12 LGB over the road intersection and the FAC painted an Iraqi tank with laser targeting energy using his hand-held Viper designator. This guided the weapon directly to the tank, which was completely destroyed in the resulting explosion. Aside from eliminating the tank, the LGB also cut a swathe through Iraqi troops who were massing around the armour in preparation for an assault on the SOF position. As the bomb impacted and Lt Caldwell climbed back up through the clouds, the FAC was jubilantly screaming the impact assessment to me over the radio. It was now my turn.

'As my aircraft accelerated along with my adrenalin, I spotted the target area and dropped my GBU-12 into the Viper's acquisition basket. The bomb guided successfully, destroying another tank and inflicting further casualties amongst the enemy troops.

'Lt Caldwell and I then orbited over the target area in cloud above the SAM MEZ as we waited for an updated assessment of the current battlefield situation. The FAC's voice had now changed tone, and he was speaking very calmly, but he was clearly still excited. Our bomb hits had helped destroy a good chunk of the Iraqi forces in the immediate vicinity of the SOF teams and the Kurdish militia, halting the enemy's advancement toward our soldiers. When Lt Caldwell asked for a situation update from the FAC, the response he got was "battlefield secured!"

'Elated that we had directly help save Coalition forces on the ground, we turned our aircraft toward the ship and headed home. The adrenalin rush was amazing, and I was completely covered in sweat. I just wanted to relax and enjoy the moment, but the effort involved in getting back to the tanker and then back aboard the ship prevented me from fully unwinding even when the weather was good, and today of course was not a good weather day.

'We soon found our KC-135 over the Iraq-Turkey border, with whom we duly repeated the never dull air-to-air refuelling aspect of our mission. We then headed west back to CVN-75, and as we flew out over the coast of Turkey we passed CVW-3 strikers bound for Iraq to perform missions similar to the one that we were now on the cusp of completing.

'It wasn't until we were "feet wet back" over the Mediterranean that the weather finally showed signs of clearing up. The patches of blue sky served as a welcome relief after flying for several hours in the clouds. It also meant that the carrier landing wouldn't be an instrument approach until a visual transition was made at roughly a quarter-of-a-mile behind the ship. That was a very good thing!'

CTF-60 attacks on Iraqi armour and troops in the Debecka Pass continued for a further 24 hours, with CVW-3 and CVW-8 dropping a considerable number of bombs on the enemy forces that had massed in the area. Although Lts Baker and Caldwell had succeeded in delivering their LGBs during the course of two low-level attack runs, JDAM ultimately proved to be the only weapon available for much of this action due to persistent cloud cover and the close proximity of the enemy to Coalition forces.

CITIES FALL

Just 24 hours after the fall of Baghdad on 10 April, Kirkuk came under Kurdish control. CTF-60 had helped pave the way for Coalition forces to enter the northern city virtually unopposed by systematically destroying Iraqi resistance in the surrounding region. Sapped of their will to fight, the thousands of troops that had pulled back into Kirkuk itself offered little resistance when the SOF troops and Kurdish Peshmerga fighters moved on the city.

To a man, the Hornet pilots were relieved that they would not have to get involved in the unpleasantness of urban CAS. Lt Cdr Blackwelder's feelings were typical of most light strike pilots embarked in the Mediterannean-based CVNs;

'If we had been called on to fly urban CAS in support of fully blown street-by-street warfare in these northern cities, I am not sure how successful we would have been when you consider how long it was taking us to find targets in open fields. With urban CAS, we would have been tasked with hitting specific buildings in city streets where every building looked the same from 20,000 ft. I can't see TACAIR ever being able to perform the urban CAS mission as effectively as a helicopter gunship.

'I personally did very little urban CAS. Indeed, the only time I dropped my bombs near a built-up area was late in the war when I attacked a chemical plant on the outskirts of Mosul. I was flying a re-strike as a follow up to a dedicated strike that had been flown earlier in the campaign.'

One of the primary reasons why light strike pilots were leery of waging war in built-up areas was that the Hornet was equipped with a targeting pod that was ill suited to this kind of tasking, as Lt Cdr Blackwelder explained;

'Virtually from the start of OEF in October 2001, the Hornet community realised that it was suffering serious target identification problems with the obsolescent NITE Hawk pod when conducting urban CAS. The replacement ASQ-228 Advanced Targeting FLIR was running late, so the "quick fix" to this problem took the form of binoculars that were issued to all light strike pilots. We were instructed to carry these in the cockpit on every mission, but I chose not to use them as there was already too much going on in the cockpit of an F/A-18 to add them to the mix – I am not a good enough pilot to deal with all of that!

'VFA-105 had started training with binoculars soon after OEF had started, but we quickly found that there was too much going on to use them in actual combat. I broke out the binoculars at Fallon during our NSAWC training, but only after I had put the auto-pilot on! I then sat back and "camped out" for a while, which is fine in a permissive environment like NSAWC, but not in a real war zone like OIF.'

Although both Mosul and Kirkuk had fallen quickly, this was not to be the case with Tikrit. The last stronghold for forces loyal to Saddam

A VFA-105 plane inspector checks the optics of the AN/AAS-38A NITE Hawk target designation pod prior to the jet being unchained and marshalled to a catapult. State-of-the-art 15 years ago, the NITE Hawk struggled in OIF, and the system is now being replaced by the ASQ-228 ATFLIR in fleet service (Cdr Tom Lalor)

Hussein's Baathist regime, and birthplace of the Iraqi President, Tikrit initially came under attack from the 1st MEF's Task Force *Tripoli* in the wake of sustained air strikes on 13 April. The following day some 250 US tanks and armoured vehicles entered the city, which was defended by Iraqi armour. More than 800 sorties were flown by Coalition aircraft supporting the assault on Tikrit, with 200 LGBs and JDAM being dropped during the course of the day. 14 April also proved to be the last time that CTF-60 expended ordnance in anger in OIF.

Both CVW-3 and CVW-8 were involved in the Tikrit operation, sharing targets with other Coalition aerial assets as Cdr Fenton of VFA-87 recalled;

'By war's end, with the attack on Tikrit, the air forces in the north and the south had started to operate alongside each other. This resulted in us being given fewer opportunities to attack targets, and the odds of anyone getting in over the city and dropping their ordnance became very small. Having said that, two of our pilots did get a tasking to take out some weapons bunkers in Tikrit itself, and they witnessed good secondary explosions after dropping their LGBs on the target.'

Capt Rainey also enjoyed a joint forces experience on 14 April;

'We worked with a number of Army FACs in OH-58D Kiowa helicopters during the final day sorties of OIF. Those guys were great at their job, and it is a real shame that they did not show up in the north until Tikrit was about to fall. They helped us take out a huge ammunition depot on the outskirts of the city, which exploded with such ferocity that you could see it going up from 100 miles away when flying in the area. The destruction of the depot came close to being an air wing "DumpEx",

The pilot of 'Canyon 412' strikes a pose for Cdr Lalor's camera en route to northern Iraq in mid April 2003. The jet's nine-bomb mission tally is clearly visible (*Cdr Tom Lalor*)

for six events went down to Tikrit to work with the Kiowa FACs. CVW-8 flew follow-up strikes on the depot that night.

'We did not work around Tikrit too much, and my particular section had actually been tasked with bombing some pre-planned targets north of Baghdad when we picked up the ammunition depot mission. We swung around the Iraqi capital, headed back north and ended up "plinking" JDAM through the weather onto the depot from 38,000 ft.

'Several days prior to this, I also conducted a mission in conjunction with a USAF E-8C J-STARS (Joint Surveillance Target Attack Radar System). We only got to work with J-STARS in the last week of the war, as prior to this they had been very busy down south.

'The Iraqis had moved 80 main battle tanks 80 miles south of Kirkuk. They were off the beaten track, hidden next to a car park. My section stumbled across them during a sortie, and a J-STARS controller confirmed that they were a legitimate target. We got a FAC on the ground to go and have a look and confirm that they were indeed tanks, and by the time the third event of the day returned to CVN-75 the Iraqi armour had been annihilated.'

Although the Iraqi Army was on the verge of defeat in OIF, fanatical elements holed up in Tikrit made sure that the city would not fall to the Coalition without a fight. Lt Cdr Metzger was a witness, and almost a victim, of this bitter rearguard action;

'I was sent down to hit a fixed target in Tikrit with JDAM on one of the last missions flown by CVW-8 in OIF. My wingman on this sortie was Lt(jg) Robert McClure, who was the junior pilot in VFA-15. We had some SAM indications on our RHAWS (Radar Homing And Warning System), but by this late stage of the war we knew that there were no missiles left in Tikrit. We later discovered that the Iraqis were actually working out our altitude in order to bracket us with AAA.

'We dropped our bombs, which hit the target, and we were heading back out of the area when AAA started to blow up all around us. A burst exploded below and in front of my jet, tossing it around like I was flying through turbulence. Fortunately, there was no damage, but it scared me to death. Looking through my NVGs, I also saw some other rounds blowing up near my wingman, and then I was dazzled by a big flash – I immediately thought that he had been hit.

'In actuality, he had seen the AAA bursting around me and pumped out an infrared decoy flare! I immediately got on the radio and asked him if he had put out a flare. He replied in the affirmative, and I shouted back, "DO NOT DO THAT AGAIN!" The flare had scared me even more than the AAA. Needless to say, he did not put out any more flares that night, and he got a stern talking to upon our return to the ship. During our debrief, I asked Lt(jg) McClure why he had shot off the flare, and he replied that he was scared.

'It was unusual, admittedly, to see AAA up at the height that we were at. Having worked out our height inbound to the target with their radar, the gunners were setting the fuses on their 105 mm shells to explode at this altitude, and we duly departed at the same height – hence the accurate bracketing.

'The Iraqi AAA gunners had seen all of our tactics over the past ten years thanks to our endless cycle of OSW deployments. The aerial aspects

Led by squadron CO Cdr Andy Lewis, all 12 of VFA-15's F/A-18Cs (the photographer is flying the 12th jet) form up for a final flypast over CVN-71 on 29 May 2003. A short while later the jets landed at NAS Oceana, Virginia, thus bringing to an end the unit's OIF war cruise (*Lt(jg) Jon Biehl*)

of OIF were effectively a repeat of *Desert Fox* in December 1998, so most Iraqi gunners were very familiar with the way we waged war from the air.'

Tikrit fell to Task Force *Tripoli* on 15 April, and for CVN-71 and CVN-75 the shooting war in the north was now over. Both CVW-3 and CVW-8 continued to maintain standing patrols over the region to discourage factional fighting between Kurdish forces and the recently defeated Iraqi troops, but no further ordnance was expended.

Harry S Truman remained in the Mediterranean until 2 May, and four days later the vessel pulled into Stokes Bay, off Portsmouth, for a three-day port call. CVW-3 departed CVN-75 just prior to the carrier docking in its home port of Norfolk, Virginia, on 23 May to bring to an end its OIF war cruise. *Theodore Roosevelt* conducted operations in the eastern Mediterranean until mid May, when it headed west to Cartegna, in Spain, for a brief port call. CVW-8 bid farewell to CVN-71 off the Virginia coast as the carrier neared Norfolk on 29 May.

The final word on just how effective the TACAIR naval aviators had been in OIF should go to Col Charles Cleveland, Commander Joint Special Operations Task Force-North. He sent the following e-mail message to CVW-3's CAG, Capt Mark Vance, and CVW-8's CAG, Capt Dave Newland, just days after major hostilities had ended;

'On behalf of Special Force A teams and the rest of us here at Task Force *Viking*, I want to say thanks for being there when we needed you. You were instrumental in our dismantling three IZ Corps and the ultimate capture of the third and fourth largest cities in Iraq. Says a lot considering the Coalition ground component largely consisted of the 10th Special Force Group (Airborne) and our Kurdish allies.

'We took some big risks knowing that when we needed you, you'd be there. You never failed us, and as a direct result, we never lost a position and had only four casualties during the entire operation. Please pass to your aircrews and their shipmates our congratulations and thanks for a job well done. Don't know when or where, but I'm sure our paths will cross again. When they do, I'll buy the beer.'

'HUNTERS" WAR

As detailed in Chapter One, CVW-8's third Hornet squadron was Reserve-manned VFA-201 'Hunters', which had been mobilised on 5 October 2002 in order to make good a short-fall in fleet-capable light strike units due to delays in the Super Hornet transition programme. Despite flying older F/A-18A+s, and being manned by 18 pilots with an average age of 35, the unit more than pulled its weight from the very moment it was assigned to CVW-8 soon after returning to active duty.

On 22 March 2003, VFA-201

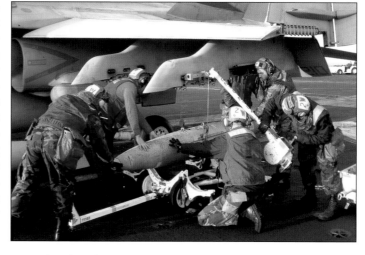

became the first Navy Reserve unit to see combat since the Korean War. Over the next 30 days, the 'Hunters' completed more than 400 combat sorties, delivered 250,127 lbs of ordnance (more than VFA-15 and VFA-87) and flew well over 1200 combat flight hours in support of OIF. Thanks to the vast experience of its pilots, VFA-201 provided no fewer than six air wing strike leaders to CVW-8 and led 30 per cent of all combat missions flown by the air wing – more than any other TACAIR unit embarked in CVN-71. Finally, the squadron's maintenance department, which was again manned by reservists, made sure that its pilots had the aircraft they required to reach a 100 per cent combat sortie completion rate. This outstanding statistic was achieved despite having to work on jets that were between 16 and 18 years old.

The 'Hunters' were thrust into combat right from the start of OIF when four aircraft were loaded with two 2000-lb GBU-31(V)2 JDAM apiece and sent off as part of CVW-8's first 'Shock and Awe' strike package on the night of 22 March. Four more identically armed F/A-18A+s were also launched on follow-up sorties 24 hours later. On both occasions military targets in Falluja were struck with clinical

VFA-201 armourers use a ubiquitous SHOLS to winch a GBU-35(V)1, fitted with a BLU-110 warhead, up from its skid onto the port outer wing pylon of 'Hunter 210' (Lot VIII F/A-18A+ BuNo 162905) during the early stages of OIF. VFA-201 dropped a total of 56 GBU-35(V)1s, 35 GBU-32(V)2s and 31 GBU-31(V)2s during the campaign. By comparison, the only JDAM weapon employed by VFA-15 and VFA-87 was the GBU-35(V)1, the 'Valions' dropping 69 and the 'War Party' 70 (*Ray Arnold*)

Two of the four VFA-201 jets that participated in CVW-8's first 'Shock and Awe' strike on 22 March 2003 are readied for a section launch from 'TR's' waist cats (*PHAN Brad Garner*)

accuracy, pilots simultaneously avoiding the large concentrations of Iraqi AAA and the occasional ballistic SAM.

Upon the jets' arrival back aboard the boat, it was clear through the FLIR footage that they had brought back with them that the 'Hunters' had completely destroyed their targets. As the unit's Public Affairs Officer (PAO), Cdr Sean Clark, described it in his official cruise summary, 'VFA-201 was clearly in the fight, and the naval reserves were actively involved and leading combat operations once again'.

Following CVW-8's brief exposure to 'Shock and Awe', CVN-71 headed north to Op Area One on 24 March after the Turkish government belatedly opened up its airspace to Coalition aircraft. KI/CAS and BAI in support of Task Force *Viking* Special Forces A teams, and their Kurdish Peshmerga allies, would now be the order of the day for the rest of OIF. Bad weather, a paucity of 'big wing' tankers, long missions and near constant night flying were all hurdles that the pilots of VFA-201 took in their stride as the unit set the pace for accurate bomb delivery and a willingness to execute any mission in their multi-role Hornets.

Mission diversity is certainly what squadron PAO Cdr Clark got during OIF. One of VFA-201's six Air Warfare Strike Commanders, he expended LGBs, JDAM, JSOW and HARM whilst completing 14 missions in 30 days of combat. Clark kept a detailed record of some of the more eventful sorties that he flew for his family back in Texas, and he has allowed the author access to this historical document.

The first mission that Cdr Clark recounted was a close air support sortie that he flew in late March, this flight being typical of the myriad

Numbered amongst VFA-201's 14 TOPGUN graduates and six Air Warfare Strike Commanders, Cdr Sean Clark is a veteran light strike pilot who has done all of his fleet flying with Pacific-based squadrons during his frontline naval career. It was therefore somewhat ironic that he actually went to war as a reservist with an east coast air wing. Cdr Clark is seen here posing with 'Hunter 212' (Lot IX F/A-18A+ BuNo 163151) (*Cdr Sean Clark*)

'Hunter 211' flies over snow-capped peaks in Kurdistan during the early stages of OIF. VFA-201 averaged more than 14 sorties a day throughout the campaign (*Lt Cdr Mark Brazelton*)

KI/CAS operations undertaken by VFA-201, and CVW-8's TACAIR units as a whole, for much of the war;

'We launched out in our normal strike packages and proceeded into country well after sunset. I checked in with our controlling agencies and was immediately assigned targets that stretched the entire width of the northern theatre. My section's assigned area was in the vicinity of Kirkuk, and was obviously right along the edge of the northern battle line. I say that based on the resistance that was encountered. Here are the details.

'My "wingee" and I checked in for tasking with our FAC team – my guess was that they were "snake eaters" who had made their way down into the thick of it. We established "comms" with them and were given some large artillery pieces to take out that had been firing at them all day – of course, the "Army", or whoever these guys were, had their interests at heart. We quickly learned that after our first run into the target area!

'My "wingee" for the night assigned each of us a large artillery piece that we were responsible for knocking out, briefed our plan of attack and verified with the FACs their precise location. Once all that was satisfied, we pressed in for our attack. Based on the position of the friendlies, we decided to run west-to-east and pull off north. My "wingee" chose to utilise the JDAM he had on board first, while I went for one of my LGBs – both weapons are equally potent against this kind of immobile threat.

'On our run inbound we quickly figured out that the FACs either a) hadn't yet seen what was there to protect the artillery pieces, or b) just neglected to tell us! In hindsight, we figured the answer was b), because it was obvious that they needed these pieces taken out for their own safety. Just when we were both at weapons release, the sky lit up with bullets coming from what we estimated to be about *ten* AAA batteries exclusively protecting the big artillery pieces.

'Now I know all of us have seen CNN footage with night vision devices of bullets shooting up in the sky – what we all haven't seen (myself included up to this point) was the same "green footage" coming over the top of your canopy and right in front of your nose. To say that I assumed the foetal position wouldn't be doing the foetal position any justice! I figured I was a goner, but that if I had come this far, with a weapon in flight, I might as well finish lasing the target so that my LGB would impact its intended receiver. I tucked down in the cockpit (not sure what good that would do, considering the shells probably would come right up my ass anyway) and squinted my eyes till the LGB obliterated the artillery piece. I then broke hard northbound and got the hell away from the area.

'I personally learned three more lessons on this particular run. 1) If you have the choice between a weapon that you can "drop and forget" or one that you have to support till impact, drop the former first. 2) It sucks to be the second guy across the same target area. And 3) The Army has some pretty frigging smart dudes! The night's story doesn't stop there though.

'Having decided that we had done enough for these guys, we went back to top off with fuel and figured that we wouldn't have to go back down to that particular part of the country again. Kind of a nice thought, considering that we had done our part that night for the guys on the ground. Well, lo and behold, when we completed tanking and punched in our coordinates for our next series of targets, we discovered that we would be heading back down to Kirkuk again!

'Our section pressed south and made the trek to a holding point just north of the target area, where my "wingee" decided that we'd just check things out to see if it had cooled down. We thought maybe the Iraqis would be taking a shwarma break or something, or had maybe lost interest in firing into the pitch black skies. Funny how you try to talk yourself into making a bad deal seem better than it is.

'Everything looked pretty quiet in the target area, and since I had the only remaining JDAM, we "cleverly" thought that I should send my weapon downrange first to see if we got a response. Probably the funniest quote of the night was my "wingee" immediately thereafter saying that he would "pass me the lead and fly high cover". Of course, I immediately said "Yeah, right, I'm sure you want to poke your nose in there!" To make a long story even longer, I took the lead and watched my "wingee" climb into the "moronosphere" to stay above any possible AAA threat known to man, while you-know-who trundled on in to stir the pot. And that's exactly what happened.

'Take our last run and multiply it by about ten! The only difference this time was that I could shuck and jive my way right into the target area, thus making it very difficult for anyone to guess where I was going to be in the next few seconds. You've got to love "drop and forget" weapons, but I just wish you could drop them about 20 miles further away. Oh, by the way, my high-flying "wingee" was providing the appropriate "holy shits" and "did you see that?" calls over the radio about every five to ten seconds. And then he had the nerve to say at the end of it all "Hey that wasn't so bad. Let's set up for my run."

'Okay, first of all, I didn't have to assume the foetal position on this particular run, but I did have some pretty good advice on what we should do next. I quote: "Let's head west towards Mosul and find some other targets". Oh, I forgot to tell you that my "wingee" for the night was a young, active-duty guy. You got to love having reservists in the air wing that know when to say when. How many guys has this "old guy" heard of getting bagged by AAA? I don't think I can count that high.

'The rest of the night really doesn't deserve print, but I must admit we dropped a lot of high explosives on "unprotected" armour west of Mosul.'

SAS RESCUE

Several nights later, Cdr Clark participated in one of VFA-201's most memorable OIF missions. The following account, which he wrote whilst performing his duties as the unit's PAO, subsequently appeared in official US naval aviation periodicals, as well as in the 'Hunters'' cruise report;

'On the night of 31 March 2003, Cdrs Sean Clark and Alan Beal, tactical call-signs "Cujo 13" and "14", launched from CVN-71 in the eastern Mediterranean. After mid-air refuelling from a KC-135 in southeastern Turkey, "Cujo 13" and "14" were told by an E-3 AWACS to proceed over 200 miles south into western Iraq and relieve a pair of USAF F-16s who had been searching for an "overrun SAS unit" for several hours – the British soldiers had been on the run for the past 30 hours. The aviators were passed a general area, given a frequency and then told that the SAS unit had infrared (IR) strobes to be visually acquired.

'Upon reaching the search area, "Cujo 13" communicated to the F-16s that he would take over search responsibilities and duly relieve them so

that they could return to their base in the Arabian Gulf region. "Cujo 13" and "14" then began their own search for the SAS unit. After roughly 30 minutes of scouring the area, "Cujo" flight picked up a faint IR strobe and started a descent to lower altitude to verify the position. Upon this verification, and subsequently marking the position of the strobe, "Cujo 13" informed the AWACS that the SAS unit had been found.

'With fuel running critically low, the F/A-18 pilots were forced to fly back to Turkish airspace to refuel. After taking on more fuel, "Cujo 13" and "14" proceeded back overhead to the SAS unit as USAF para-rescue forces were launched to retrieve the British troops.

'While overhead the SAS unit, "Cujo 13" and "14" detected Iraqi Army vehicles driving towards the search area. The Iraqis were also looking for this overrun unit, and they began searching in close proximity to the SAS squad with flashlights. Sensing that the Iraqi Army was getting too close to the SAS unit, "Cujo" flight made it perfectly clear to the pursuing enemy troops on the ground that they should abandon their search and depart the area. Setting up a circular pattern over the Iraqis, "Cujo" flight began a series of threatening passes to scare off the soldiers. Believing that they might be attacked, the Iraqis retreated, got back in their vehicles and drove out of the search area.

'After approximately 40 minutes, USAF para-rescue units, escorted by A-10s, appeared on station to retrieve the SAS unit. "Cujo 13" and "14" remained overhead the rescue effort to provide CAS should the need arise to suppress any further Iraqi advances. Soon reaching extremely critical fuel levels, "Cujo 13" and "14" passed the suppression role over to the A-10s, whose pilots had now visually acquired the SAS unit.

'After seven hours of flight time, and recovery aboard CVN-71, "Cujo" flight learned that the SAS unit was safely back in Coalition hands. The British troops had been inserted in western Iraq early in the war to secure an area suspected of housing Scud missiles. Soon after the start of hostilities, the SAS unit's position was compromised and the Iraqis began to overrun the area. The soldiers had been forced to retreat into central Iraq and fend off a significant enemy force that was hunting them down.

'Both VFA-201 pilots earned their pay on this particular mission.'

Cdr Clark was back over northern Iraq once again 24 hours later;

'My "wingee" and I checked in with our controlling agency, looking for tasking, and we were told to contact a FAC in the far eastern part of the

The pilot of 'Hunter 205' (Lot VIII F/A-18A+ BuNo 162886) goes in search of the increasingly elusive enemy soon after dawn on 14 April 2003. Having failed to drop any ordnance during the previous 72 hours due to a lack of credible targets, CVW-8 expended its final 23 bombs (six GBU-32(V)2s and 17 GBU-12s) of OIF on this date during the battle for Tikrit (*Lt Cdr Mark Brazelton*)

country. We established radio contact with a guy on the ground who sounded like he was about 13 years old! In fact, I was really starting to doubt whether we had the correct frequency, and that some kid in America had figured out a way to tap into our most secure communications network. I quickly changed my mind, however, when we heard the sounds of incoming artillery shells and the yelling of his buddies to take cover. No kid can find that kind of background "music".

'We quickly received a 9-line attack brief, which was basically a summary of what we were attacking, who was where on the battlefield and a time that the guy on the ground wanted us to arrive overhead. I must caveat all this by saying that there were a few choice expletives thrown in for good "Army" measure – a definite sign that these guys were in the "shit". Another good sign was the time that these guys wanted us to arrive. I quote, "Time on target – as soon as you can get here".

'Our target for the night was a series of artillery batteries that the Iraqis had set up on a unique ridgeline in the northern theatre. Now you might think that if something is on a ridgeline, it must be easy to see? Well, you've got to remember that it's about 0200 hrs, and man wasn't supposed to be up at this time of night – least not on a battlefield, trying to find the proverbial "needle in the haystack".

'My "wingee" and I had a pretty good idea of the topography of the ridgeline that the FAC was talking about, and we decided that we would

'Hunter 200' was easily the most colourful jet to grace 'TR's' flightdeck during OIF, the VFA-201 CAG jet even boasting a candy-striped tailhook! But the aircraft was much more than just a 'show pony', as it ended OIF with a bomb tally consisting of 15 LGB/JDAM and no less than five HARM silhouettes. This photograph was taken during a post-dawn mission in the first week of April 2003, when CTF-60 CAS strikes were at their peak in northern Iraq – CVW-8 dropped no fewer than 158 GBU-12s and 97 GBU-35(V)1s between 1 and 5 April (*Lt Cdr Mark Brazelton*)

The pilot of 'Hunter 213' (Lot VIII F/A-18A+ BuNo 162861) cruises over rugged terrain as he heads for Kirkuk on 11 April 2003. The jet failed to find any tasking on this mission and duly made the long flight back to CVN-71 with its LGBs still aboard (*Lt Cdr Mark Brazelton*)

start by placing one bomb somewhere in the middle of it and then have him talk us either east or west to the artillery pieces. It's amazing how quickly you think on your feet in war.

'We confirmed the position of the FACs and then dropped a bomb directly in the middle of the ridgeline at its highest point. Little did we know that the Iraqis were also using this same high ground as an observation post – clearly evident in our FLIR pod as we approached closer to the target. Well, as luck would have it, the Iraqis had lost their "eyes" for directing the artillery fire, we had gained a position from which the FACs could now target us onto the pieces themselves, and we probably took out a couple of bad guys who knew something about directing fire support. All of these things were good.

'My "wingee" and I then circled back around with the guidance of the FACs and began moving our ordnance systematically up and down the ridgeline, targeting the specific weapons that had been firing at them. We had clearly made these guys' day, and they were more than thankful that we had taken out two or three large artillery pieces. They said their goodbyes and wished us "happy landings". We turned our Hornets westward, started our climb and began the whole thought process that goes through any naval aviator's mind at night – the dreaded night landing!

'Now, you'd think that after doing all that "war stuff" we could just sit back and enjoy the hour-and-a-half trip back to the boat. But I'm here to tell you that the fear of flying over Iraq doesn't compare to having to land back aboard that floating "postage stamp". And to make matters worse, the boat was always finding the worst weather – something about the wind and such! That night the skies were not only pitch black, but the boat was also sailing into some really awful weather. Man, what I wouldn't have given for an 8000-ft runway – those Air Force guys really have got it made.

'I checked in with the boat and started my descent on down. The clouds and lightning were all around and the jet was getting quite a buffeting from the turbulence. This, in turn, created a major case of vertigo. I literally felt like I was flying inverted!

'I started my level off at 1200 ft and eight miles behind the boat – normally about the same time you would start to "see" the boat on a dark, dark, night. Well, not tonight. In fact, I wouldn't "see" the boat until around three-quarters of a mile, and that same buffeting from turbulence was still kicking in at 300 ft! I began to think that I was just a voting member in the aircraft, and not the guy flying it – a not so comforting feeling. The latter, I suppose, has something to do with this night carrier landing stuff, as you either land or you die!

'Now I know that sounds dramatic, but it is also reality. I think more than that though, the fear of looking bad in front of your peers somehow keeps you in check and helps you do whatever it takes to land safely – not to mention the real chance that you could die.

'I somehow managed to get aboard the boat, and I think I may have held my breath for the last 15 to 20 seconds of my approach before my tailhook grabbed the arresting wire. I taxied clear and, when I finally shut the jet down, literally sat there in the cockpit for a good three minutes waiting for my legs to stop shaking. I can count on one hand the times during my career as a naval aviator that this has happened, and the episode on 1 April 2003 probably takes the cake!'

LMAV

Although the venerable AGM-65E laser Maverick proved to be an extremely popular urban and battlefield CAS weapon with Marine Air Group 11 in Kuwait and the NAG-based Hornet units during OIF, it was only employed once by CTF-60. That honour went to VFA-201 on 10 April, and Cdr Clark was responsible for working up the target set for this mission. He described the unique sortie in the following journal entry;

'This sortie demonstrated the lengths to which Saddam's regime would go to protect important military assets. It also showed how far our Coalition forces were going to protect innocent civilians from being needlessly harmed.

'I was standing my duty as the Air Warfare Strike Commander when I received a series of coordinates and target photos from CENTCOM in the general area of downtown Tikrit. The target was labelled as the "number one mobile target for the day in the entire theatre of operations", and was also described as a Time Sensitive Target. This generally meant that the enemy would probably be moving it quite frequently to try and protect it from being bombed.

'Well, it seems that the Iraqis had placed a military communications van in the downtown area of the city, this particular vehicle being used by Army staff officers to communicate with their troops surrounding Tikrit. Coalition forces had literally homed in on it after picking up numerous transmissions from this area. A "sensor" was then tasked with overflying the area to take digital photography and gather precise target coordinates.

'I had just completed reading our explicit instructions on the target, and asked the air wing targeteer to come over and help me in the assessment of the target area photos when, to our utter amazement, we opened the target folder and saw the van sitting in the middle of the Tikrit Amusement Park! The target was literally between the roller coaster and the Ferris wheel. It seems that Saddam was going to try and keep this target from being hit by using innocent people as shields during the day and then camouflage the target at night so that we wouldn't see it.

'Our instructions were to "destroy" this target, but to min-imise all collateral damage to the surrounding area. We were also instructed to employ a weapon that had only a minimal blast fragmenta-tion pattern. These instructions alone drove us to use the only weapon designed for this type of tar-get – an AGM-65E laser Maverick.

'With our marching orders in hand, I asked our Intel folks to give me the missile order of battle for the downtown Tikrit area, and I imme-diately saw that there were numer-ous Iraqi SAM batteries still

'Hunter 203' boasted a unique mission tally for a CTF-60 Hornet, as it was the only jet in the northern campaign to employ an AGM-65 laser Maverick missile in anger in OIF. Each bomb marked up on a VFA-201 Hornet signified one mission on which that aircraft had expended either LGBs, JDAM or JSOW. Cdr Sean Clark recalled 'We figured that if we applied one bomb symbol for each individual weapon that we expended, we'd soon run out of room on the aircraft! On each mission we dropped roughly three bombs – two JDAM and one LGB, or vice versa'. The HARM silhouettes, however, represent a single AGM-88 fired (*Lt Cdr Mark Brazelton*)

The urban CAS weapon of choice for US TACAIR, the AGM-65E laser Maverick missile has recently seen combat in Kosovo, Afghanistan and Iraq. Only a single round was fired in northern Iraq, however, VFA-201 destroying a communications truck in central Tikrit on 10 April 2003 (*PHAN Kristopher Wilson*)

An F-14D from VF-213 provided laser guidance for VFA-201's LMAV shot on 10 April using its superior LTS pod. This was the one and only occasion in OIF where a 'Black Lions' Tomcat buddy-lased for a CVW-8 Hornet. Here, a section of VFA-201 jets prepare to launch with a JDAM-armed F-14D on 2 April 2003 (*PH2 James K McNeil*)

The 'Hunters' of 2003. Note the jet's air brake, adorned with a full colour First Navy Jack (*VFA-201*)

protecting the city. This strike was going to be a high risk, pinpoint attack, and it needed our best people behind the trigger.

'I assigned the target to the strike lead that was just about ready to start his brief, and passed him all the information that I had on the van, and its immediate surroundings. I also informed him on the choice of weapon, and why this target could only be struck with a Maverick missile. He agreed with me on the weapon, and I then notified the ordnance department to bring up an AGM-65E to the flight deck. The weapon was then uploaded onto "Hunter 203" (BuNo 162856) and readied for flight.

'The strike package proceeded into Iraq after their two-hour trek across southern Turkey. It was approximately 0200 hrs when they arrived in the

vicinity of Tikrit, by which point the amusement park was well past its closing time. With precise coordinates in hand, it was decided that a LANTIRN pod-equipped F-14D from VF-213 would provide the laser energy for the AGM-65 – this was the only time that a Tomcat "buddy-lased" for a Hornet from CVW-8 during the entire campaign.

'The VFA-201 jet, flown by Lt Cdr John Mooney, would dive into the "hornets' nest", acquire the target and fire the LMAV while avoiding the AAA batteries and SAM sites that ringed Tikrit. Providing SEAD support were two F/A-18Cs from VFA-15 and an EA-6B from VAQ-141.

'The attack went off without a hitch, Lt Cdr Mooney miraculously finding the target in darkened Tikrit and knocking it out with a direct hit from the LMAV. The van was destroyed and the collateral damage was limited to the target itself. There were no subsequent reports of civilian casualties, and having achieved complete surprise, the aircraft escaped the heavily defended city virtually without a shot being fired at them.

'The imagery brought back of the strike's execution was nothing short of phenomenal. The "Hunters" had once again delivered a dynamic punch to the Iraqi Army just when it was needed most, the LMAV removing a major portion of the command and control ability of the forces in Tikrit. The city itself fell into Coalition hands four days later.'

On 29 May 2003, all 12 F/A-18A+s departed CVN-71 for the last time and flew back to VFA-201's NAS/JRB Fort Worth home, thus ending an historic cruise for the naval reservists. The squadron had left Texas on 5 January expecting a four-week 'at sea period' and had actually been thrust into a five-month 'extended' deployment in support of OIF. Demobilised soon after its return to the US, VFA-201 reverted to its adversary role once again. The unit's contribution to OIF was aptly summarised as follows by Cdr Clark for VFA-201's cruise report;

'The "Hunters" answered the call to duty over the past year and provided the kind of response that the active duty Navy can expect from its Reserve force. If the need should arise in the future to once again flex its muscles, the country should rest assured that it can call on the "Hunters" and activate an extremely professional fighting force.

'We came, we fought, we kicked some major ass!'

'Hunter 200', with squadron CO Cdr Tom Marotta at the controls, leads a four-ship flypast of CVN-71 as VFA-201 depart the carrier and head for Texas on 29 May 2003 (*Lt Cdr Mark Brazelton*)

APPENDICES

US NAVY OP AREA ONE-BASED F/A-18 HORNETS INVOLVED IN OIF

CVW-3 (USS *HARRY S TRUMAN* (CVN-75))

VFA-37 'BULLS' (F/A-18C)

165181/300	165184/306
165177/301	165171/307
165183/302	165175/310
165199/303	165185/311
165182/304	165176/312
165179/305	165204/314

VFA-105 'GUNSLINGERS' (F/A-18C)

164200/400	164197/406
164261/401	164253/407
164236/402	164246/410
164243/403	164231/411
164244/404	164215/412
164238/405	164235/413

CVW-8 (USS *THEODORE ROOSEVELT* (CVN-71))

VFA-201 'HUNTERS' (F/A-18A+)

162904/200	162888/206
162834/201	162899/207
162841/202	162905/210
162856/203	163113/211
162859/204	163151/212
162886/205	162861/213

VFA-15 'VALIONS' (F/A-18C)

164627/300	164691/306
164629/301	164689/307
164643/302	164673/310
164646/303	164680/311
164655/304	164631/312
164661/305	164657/314

VFA-87 'GOLDEN WARRIORS' (F/A-18C)

164687/400	164644/406
164675/401	164628/407
164647/402	164632/410
164663/403	164669/411
164671/404	164252/412
164630/405	164205/414

COLOUR PLATES

1

F/A-18C BuNo 165181 of VFA-37, USS *Harry S Truman* (CVN-75), Mediterranean Sea, March 2003
Delivered new to VFA-37 in 1995, this aircraft initially served as 'Bull 311' until it replaced BuNo 165182 as the squadron's CAG jet in 2000. 'Bull 300' was rarely seen without its blue-striped tanks during OIF. VFA-37 chose not to mark its aircraft up with bomb tallies during the conflict.

2

F/A-18C BuNo 165177 of VFA-37, USS *Harry S Truman* (CVN-75), Mediterranean Sea, April 2003
This aircraft was also delivered to VFA-37 in 1995, becoming 'Bull 314'. It too received a 'high-vis' scheme in 2000 when it became the CO's aircraft in place of BuNo 165199. VFA-37 is unique in the light strike world for applying different squadron emblems to its two colour jets, 'Bull 301' featuring the unit's original bull's head design. The Hornet also boasts detail markings in red, rather than blue.

3

F/A-18C BuNo 165185 of VFA-37, USS *Harry S Truman* (CVN-75), Mediterranean Sea, April 2003
Ten of VFA-37's 12 F/A-18Cs featured standard low-visibility markings as seen here on 'Bull 311', which has served with the unit for the past ten years. Like the rest of the Hornets currently flown by VFA-37, it initially saw combat in Operation *Desert Fox* in 1998 and then played a key role in Operation *Southern Watch* in 2000-01.

4

F/A-18C BuNo 164200 of VFA-105, USS *Harry S Truman* (CVN-75), Mediterranean Sea, April 2003
The most colourful Hornet in CTF-60 had to be 'Canyon 400', which also boasted a highly detailed mission log on its nose. VFA-105's maintainers diligently applied ordnance silhouettes to their jets from early April onwards, producing detailed stencils for JDAM, LGBs, JSOW and HARM. Each silhouette also featured the date on which the weapon was expended. This style of marking had first appeared on 'Gunslinger' Hornets in the aftermath of *Desert Fox*. BuNo 164200 was delivered new to VFA-105 in September 1990 when the unit transitioned from A-7Es to F/A-18Cs. It has been the unit's CAG jet ever since.

5

F/A-18C BuNo 164261 of VFA-105, USS *Harry S Truman* (CVN-75), Mediterranean Sea, April 2003
Just as colourful as 'Canyon 400', BuNo 164261 has also been the unit's '401' jet since its delivery to the squadron in September 1990. The President Harry S Truman-inspired *"GIVE'EM HELL!"* titling on the Hornet's nose was worn by a number of aircraft in CVW-3. Other detail markings present on VFA-105 jets included the motto *Warheads on Foreheads!* in

green on the jet's LERX and the initials *FFGFYG* (Fist Fight Go For Your Gun) on the LERX fences.

6

F/A-18C BuNo 164231 of VFA-105, USS *Harry S Truman* (CVN-75), Mediterranean Sea, April 2003

The ten 'low-vis' F/A-18Cs flown by VFA-105 in OIF also exhibited the numerous detail markings worn by the unit's colour jets, but in shades of grey rather than green and yellow. 'Canyon 411' found itself in the thick of the action, ending the campaign with five LGB, six JDAM and two JSOW silhouettes painted on its nose. Delivered new to VFA-131 in December 1990, this jet was transferred to VFA-105 12 years later following a brief spell in storage.

7

F/A-18C BuNo 164627 of VFA-15, USS *Theodore Roosevelt* (CVN-71), Mediterranean Sea, March 2003

Like VFA-37 aboard CVN-75, VFA-15 chose not to adorn its jets with bomb tallies – unit CO Cdr Andy Lewis told the author that to have asked his hard-pressed maintainers to adorn his squadron's 12 Hornets with mission markings would have made their 16- to 18-hour working days longer still. Aside from its full colour tail markings, 'Valion 300' also featured a red and white First Navy Jack, adorned with a rattlesnake and the motto *DON'T TREAD ON ME*. The Jack was first flown by Commodore Esek Hopkins in the autumn of 1775 as he readied the Continental Navy in the Delaware River during the War of Independence. His signal for the whole fleet to engage the enemy was the striped Jack. In late 2001 the Chief of Naval Operations directed that the First Navy Jack be flown on all US Navy ships in lieu of the Union Jack during the Global War on Terrorism to honour those who had died during the attacks of 11 September 2001. Delivered new to VFA-15 in September 1991, BuNo 164627 has served exclusively as 'Valion 300' for the past 14 years. Aside from combat in OIF, the jet also participated in the early OEF strikes of October-November 2001, when CVW-8 was embarked in USS *Enterprise* (CVN-65).

8

F/A-18C BuNo 164643 of VFA-15, USS *Theodore Roosevelt* (CVN-71), Mediterranean Sea, March 2003

'Valion 302' was flown by nugget pilot Lt(jg) Jon Biehl on his first OIF mission on 26 March 2003, this aircraft being one of four VFA-15 F/A-18Cs sortied by the unit as part of CVW-8's DCA support package for the 173rd Airborne Brigade's assault on Bashur air base. Like 'Valion 300', BuNo 164643 (assigned to squadron XO Cdr Ed Langford) featured a First Navy Jack but in 'low-vis' greys, as well as a wrench symbol behind the cockpit. The latter emblem denoted that VFA-15's maintenance department had been selected as the 2002 Strike Fighter Wing Atlantic Maintenance Department of the Year. The winning of this award meant that the unit could adorn each of its Hornets with the coveted wrench symbol for a full year, with 'Valion 300' and '301' having this marking applied in gold.

9

F/A-18C BuNo 164687 of VFA-87, USS *Theodore Roosevelt* (CVN-71), Mediterranean Sea, April 2003

VFA-87 chose to mark its jets with bomb tallies during OEF (this particular Hornet bore 11 silhouettes upon its return to NAS Oceana in November 2001), and the unit continued with this tradition in 2003. For the Afghanistan operation, simple bomb symbols had been applied beneath *OPERATION ENDURING FREEDOM* titling, but for OIF the bombs were replaced by tomahawks in correct 'War Party' style, as well as the titling *OPERATION IRAQI FREEDOM*. 'Party 400' had completed 26 bombing missions by war's end, this tally being bettered only by 'Party 403' with 31. Delivered new to VFA-87 in July 1992, BuNo 164687 became the unit's CAG jet in late 2000.

10

F/A-18C BuNo 164669 of VFA-87, USS *Theodore Roosevelt* (CVN-71), Mediterranean Sea, April 2003

Nicknamed the *ULTIMATE WARRIOR* in honour of television starlet Xena the Warrior Princess, the jet has carried this unique titling since its OEF cruise of 2001. Marked up with eight bomb symbols in the wake of its exploits over Afghanistan, BuNo 164669 boasted 17 hatchets upon its return home from OIF in May 2003.

11

F/A-18A+ BuNo 162904 of VFA-201, USS *Theodore Roosevelt* (CVN-71), Mediterranean Sea, April 2003

Delivered to the Navy in October 1986, this aircraft was subsequently issued to VFA-151 as the Japan-based unit switched from the F-4S to the F/A-18A. A veteran of *Desert Storm*, the jet returned to CONUS in mid 1991 when VFA-151 replaced its A-models with F/A-18Cs. Assigned to Reserve-manned VFA-203 at NAS Cecil Field, Florida, in 1996, the fighter was one of around 200 A-models upgraded to A+ standard in 2001-02. It was passed on to VFA-201 in the autumn of 2002 and marked up as the unit's CAG jet.

12

F/A-18A+ BuNo 162856 of VFA-201, USS *Theodore Roosevelt* (CVN-71), Mediterranean Sea, April 2003

Assigned to Cdr Sean Clark, 'Hunter 203' boasted a unique mission tally for a CTF-60 Hornet, as it was the only jet in the northern campaign to employ an AGM-65 laser Maverick missile in anger in OIF. Delivered to the Navy in February 1986, this aircraft served with fleet replacement squadron VFA-125 at NAS Lemoore immediately prior to it being upgraded to F/A-18A+ standard in 2002 and issued to VFA-201 in September of that year. BuNo 162856 remains in service with the 'Hunters' today.

INDEX

References to illustrations are shown in **bold**. Plates are shown with page and caption locators in brackets, with 'insignia' plates having an 'I' prefix.